AFTER THE STORMS

FROM RED DIRT TO REDEMPTION

S.E. CUNNINGHAM
FOREWORD BY ANDREW WOMMACK

RHORDIN PUBLISHING

"One of the greatest gifts a book can offer is the chance to step into someone else's life—and Stevan has lived several lifetimes in one. In these pages you'll get hit by a tornado and an earthquake, survive the rigors of boot camp, deploy to Iraq, and step into the high-risk world of undercover narcotics work and wrestle with the shadow of death. It's a journey through danger, discipline and the faithfulness of God. This book will expand your world."

— Lance Wallnau, Author, Teacher, Minister

"This book delivers a raw, hope-filled memoir that reads like a rescue story—one family, one faith, and one determined man learning, again and again, that storms don't get the final word. With vivid scenes from red-dirt Oklahoma to the crucible of military life, Cunningham writes with honesty about loss, poverty, and hardship, while never losing sight of the steady thread of redemption running through every chapter. This is a compelling testament to the power of perseverance and the grace that meets us in the wreckage—and it will leave readers encouraged that what was broken can be rebuilt."

— Phil Kassel, Author of *Grace Fueled GRIT*

To Mom.

CONTENTS

FOREWORD

I met S. E. Cunningham through my niece many years ago. I have visited with him many times and even stayed in his home. We've shared laughs and heartaches together, and I've been impressed with everything I've seen. I've ministered in his church and seen the anointing of God on his life and ministry. He has gained a stability and maturity in a lot shorter time than I was able to acquire it.

I've heard bits and pieces of the stories he relates in this book, but I can honestly say, I was amazed as I read his account of all the things he's been through in his life. I had no idea of the depth of the challenges he has dealt with. He has come through all those things without the smell of smoke. Only the Lord could do that.

I am amazed at the clarity he had to express all he's dealt with in his life. He's an excellent writer and the way he communicates holds your attention, making you want to hear more.

I believe the Lord inspired him to write this book and anointed him to describe all life threw at him in such a way that every person reading this can relate. Although I haven't traveled the same road he did, I found lots of feelings and emotions that I connected to my own journey. I've had a very easy life compared to S.E., but as I read this book, I found myself gaining insight on how to look at things in my own life and how to navigate through them the way the Lord inspired him to.

Although every person's life is unique, Paul said in 1 Corinthians. 10:13, there aren't unique temptations. We all fight the same battles to find significance, identity, purpose, and how to deal with all life throws at us. S.E. was able to articulate his journey with such precision that it helped bring my own life into focus and gave me more compassion towards others who have not been as fortunate.

I highly recommend this book and its author. Testimonies are inspiring and S.E. has a testimony that deserves to be read. When you see someone who has been through things that are worse than you've had to deal with, it helps shrink your problems down in size. If the Lord can bring this man to where he is today, He can do the same for you.

One of the themes of S.E.'s testimony is the unfailing love and faithfulness of God. Even when it seems like God is far away, He never leaves us or forsakes us and can work any negative thing in your life together for something good, if you allow Him to. It doesn't happen automatically. You have to cooperate by turning to Him and giving Him a chance. This testimony could be that connection you need to find your own way through your storm.

—Andrew Wommack, Woodland Park, Colorado

INTRODUCTION

This is the story of my walk—a journey shaped by experience and grounded in faith. I know we may not share the same starting point or beliefs, but I want to offer a glimpse into a reality that changed me. For years, life broke me—physically, mentally, and spiritually. Yet, through trial and error, I found hope in the darkness. I learned that only my faith had the strength to carry me through.

I am sharing this because I want you to see that the hardest hits do not have to be the end of your story. There is a tangible grace, an overwhelming peace, and an eventual victory waiting on the other side of the struggle.

I am offering a living testament to the hope and strength that are available to anyone who seeks them. This story is an invitation—an opportunity to witness the freedom I found and to see what is possible should you choose to walk this same transformative road I walked...

from **Red Dirt to Redemption.**

1

THE WEIGHT OF THE GREEN SKY

In Southwestern Oklahoma, you grow up knowing that the wind is not just weather—it is a force that can negotiate with your life. It is a living, breathing entity that stalks the plains, sometimes whispering through the buffalo grass and other times screaming with a fury that shakes the bedrock of the Wichita Mountains. Growing up, you learn to read the sky like a book of prophecy. You learn the difference between a "rain smell" and the metallic, ozone scent of a sky preparing to tear itself open. April 10, 1979, was the day the negotiations ended in Lawton, Oklahoma.

The sky that afternoon did not just turn dark; it turned a bruised, sickly shade of green—a color that signaled the atmosphere was no longer interested in peace. In that part of the country, we call it "tornado weather," but that sterile term does not capture the dread of watching the horizon begin to rotate. It was the kind of day where the birds go silent, and the air becomes so heavy it feels like you are breathing underwater.

On that Tuesday, the wind stopped whispering and began howling with predatory intent. For those of us on the ground, the Wichita Mountains were no longer just a beautiful backdrop; they were witnesses to a storm that would redefine the meaning of "home." We learned that day that while the wind can negotiate, it can also take everything you own in a matter of seconds, leaving you with nothing but the ground you stand on and the faith you carry in your heart. It was a baptism by wind and debris, a moment that carved into me the reality that our physical foundations are fragile, and our only true security lies in the Unshakable.

The Caboose of the Lineage

To understand the man I am today, you must first understand the giants I stood behind and the lessons I gathered from their shadows. I was the youngest of eight children—the "caboose" of a long, heavy train that had been chugging across a rugged landscape for decades. This train had endured many hard winters and navigated countless lean harvests long before I ever took my first breath. By the time I arrived, the air was already thick with the stories of those who had come before me; the family identity was no longer a fresh trail, but a well-worn path through the wilderness.

In a family that size, you quickly realize the tracks are already laid. You are not just an individual; you are a vital part of a massive, moving engine of history. The momentum of my older siblings— their successes, failures, and sacrifices—determined the speed at which I traveled. I did not have to build the road, but I had to learn to keep pace with a force that was already at full steam. Being the caboose offered a unique vantage point: I could see exactly where we had been, even as I was pulled toward an uncertain future by the sheer weight of my family's past.

A Fractured Light

There is a specific perspective that comes with being last in line. My brothers and sisters saw our early years through different eyes, and I have no intention of disputing their truths. Memory is a fractured thing, like light hitting a diamond; we each occupied a different seat at the table, and the view is unique from every angle. Over time, I have come to cherish both our differences and our similarities alike, recognizing the unique value each sibling brings to my story. Looking back through the lens of experience, God strategically surrounded me with amazing people throughout my life. It was as if He were placing a hedge of protection around me, ensuring I was shielded even when the storms of life were at their absolute worst. Some of my siblings may have seen the hunger more clearly than I did, the silence of empty cupboards echoing louder in their ears. Others felt the crushing weight of manual labor more heavily, their backs bending under a midday sun while I was still just learning to walk. They withstood the worst of the "lean years" so that by the time the resources reached me, the edge had been taken off the struggle.

Shadows and Shields

I was wrapped in the protective, fierce love of those who came before me, shielded by a wall of older siblings who had already learned how to take a hit so I would not have to. To be the youngest was a dual inheritance: I was the recipient of a vast, collective wisdom, but I was also the witness to a struggle that had been raging long before my arrival.

I stepped into a story that was already in mid-sentence, a narrative of survival well underway. My older siblings had already faced the giants and walked through the fires. I was the one who got to watch how they fought, how they bled, and—most importantly—how they refused to stay down. Their endurance became my blueprint. I learned how to handle obstacles by watching their movements before I ever put on a uniform. I saw the fight in their eyes and the resilience in my mother's hands. This is the story of how that "caboose" eventually found its own engine and its own mission, guided by the

Sovereign hands that held me when I was small and the invisible thread of grace that pulled me toward my own horizon.

A Foundation of Faith

The defining thread that runs through the very fabric of my family is our shared love of God.

This spiritual foundation began with my mother. She was the intentional architect of our faith. She made sure we truly knew Him and understood the amazing sacrifice Jesus made for us on the cross. In a world that often feels chaotic, she was the anchor that kept our family together when everything else seemed set on tearing us apart.

Her steadfast love for God was more than just a sentiment; it was a pillar of strength.

She had a fierce, God-given will that refused to let our circumstances dictate our outcome, and it is that very resilience that made us who we are today.

Mom was born in 1929 and raised in a tiny speck on the map called Francis, Oklahoma. She was old enough to carry the memories of the Dust Bowl, coming of age while the Great Depression raged across the heartland. We often heard her describe her childhood home—a place so weather-beaten and porous that it had holes in the floor, where pigs and chickens from outside would root around underneath the house.

She spent much of her teenage years stooped in the fields, picking cotton under the relentless sun to help the family make ends meet. In those long rows, amid the windswept Oklahoma plains, her "never-give-up" attitude was forged. That resilience became the iron in her blood. She fought fiercely through the toughest, most bitter seasons, driven by a mission to provide for her children. She faced trials with rare and powerful balance: a firm hand offering discipline and direction, and a soft heart giving a sanctum of love.

Her life was my first hard lesson in endurance. She showed me not to stop when tired; you stop only when the job is done. The fortitude she built in Oklahoma's cotton fields became our family's foundation. She did not just survive the Dust Bowl and the Depression. She let those trials refine her into a protector who tried to shield all her children from the storms of our own lives.

Through her example, I learned to walk a path of love, grace, and kindness grounded in biblical principles. We willingly followed that path because of the light she reflected. She did not just tell us about the Gospel. She modeled it in the way she handled lean years and loud storms. Her life was a living invitation to trust in something greater than our own strength.

However, as you will read in the chapters ahead, there were other times when I chose to stray and do my own thing. I allowed myself to be led by my own fleeting desires and impulsive instincts rather than His perfect will. Like a soldier wandering off mission into unsecured territory, I tested the boundaries of that foundation, pushing against the very truths that were meant to protect me.

Yet, even in my most reckless wandering, the strength I had seen in my mother—and the God she served with such fierce devotion— never wavered. Her faith was not a fair-weather conviction; it was a reinforced shelter that could weather any storm.

Through every high and low, God has remained constant—the steady, immovable foundation, unchanged regardless of the chaos around us. Her strength taught me where to look for mine. She made sure that even when I lost my way, even when I drifted off-course and was blinded by my own dust, I always knew where "Home" was. She did not just build a house. She built a spiritual landmark I could always return to, no matter how dark the night.

2

THE LINEAGE

Ronnie was the firstborn of the eight children brought into this world by Lavada (or LV as everyone called her) and J.R. Cunningham—the man and woman I simply knew as Mom and Dad. Ronnie was the pioneer of our sibling group, the head of our family line, arriving long before I was even a thought, let alone a distant hope, in my parents' minds.

Tragically, his time on this earth was fleeting; he passed away a mere five years after his birth, leaving a void that the years could never quite fill. Though I never had the opportunity to meet him in this life, feel his presence, or hear his laughter firsthand, Ronnie's impact on our family remains a constant, quiet hum in the background of our daily lives. He is an indelible part of our story—a chapter written in the heavy ink of sorrow yet illuminated by the golden light of hope.

His absence shaped the atmosphere of our home in ways I only began to understand as I grew older. It was a phantom pain that my parents carried, a silent reminder of the fragility of life. Yet, because of the unwavering foundation of faith my mother instilled in us, I do not mourn as those who have no hope. Instead, I live with the blessed assurance that our introduction is merely delayed, not denied. I know with absolute certainty that one day, when the storms of this life are finally stilled and the final watch is over, we will be reunited in heaven. On that day, the "caboose" will finally catch up to the pioneer, and I will finally get to know the brother who started it all. Until then, his memory serves as a reminder that our true home is not found in the red dirt of Oklahoma, but in the presence of the Father.

The Rock

Jackie was next in the sibling line, a mere two years old when the family suffered the devastating and life-altering loss of Ronnie. By the time I finally entered the world, the age gap was significant; he was already a man, sixteen years my senior, standing on the threshold of his own destiny. Shortly after my birth, he enlisted, transitioning from the red dirt of Oklahoma to the disciplined ranks of the military, where he became a permanent, formidable fixture in the United States Army.

To me, Jackie was not just an older brother wearing a uniform; he was the living, breathing embodiment of what a soldier should be—disciplined, steady, and an immovable presence in a world that often felt like it was shifting and crumbling beneath our feet. In our neighborhood and environment, where the winds of chaos often threatened to sweep people away, Jackie was the bulwark that held us fast to the shoreline.

He carried himself with a quiet authority that did not need to shout to be heard. His commitment to service was not just a career choice; it was a character trait that provided a blueprint for my own future. Watching him, I learned that a man's strength is not measured by his ability to cause a commotion, but by his ability to remain standing when the storm is at its peak. He represented a standard of excellence that felt both legendary and attainable, proving to a young "caboose" like me that you could wear the weight of responsibility and still move with purpose and grace.

Pillars of the Family

He and his wife, Debbie, became the steady, sturdy pillars of our family. They were the hands that stayed busy, constantly finding ways to support Mom and Dad whenever the burdens of life grew too heavy to bear alone. They did not squander their precious free time on personal leisure; instead, they invested it in the household. I have countless memories of them sitting at our kitchen table with mom and dad for hours on end, the air filled with the familiar snap of shuffling cards or the sound of dominoes hitting the old, worn playing surface. In those simple games, they provided us with the very thing we craved: stability and a sense of belonging. It was not always for the good times, though. Whenever my dad would go on a "binge," the atmosphere of our home shifted from stability to a familiar, frantic survival mode. It was in those moments, watching Jackie navigate my father's condition with steady hands, that I saw a different kind of soldiering—one that did not happen on a battlefield, but in the confines of our home. Jackie and Debbie bore a burden that was far too heavy for Mom to carry alone, ensuring that even during a binge, the family did not lose its way.

On our birthdays, Jackie and Debbie made a deliberate, loving effort to ensure we felt seen and valued. In a childhood where so much of what we owned was secondhand or provided by charity, the gifts they brought us were different. These were not items pulled from a dusty donation bin or handed out at a local community center; they were brand new, chosen specifically for us. Those gifts did more than provide entertainment—they restored a rare and precious sense of dignity. They taught us that we were worth the effort, and that we were not just "cases" to be managed by the system, but children to be celebrated.

A Legacy of Service

The military legacy Jackie established came full circle years later. By the time I was assigned to Fort Sill, Jackie was still serving—a seasoned veteran of the path I was only beginning to walk. When the day finally arrived for me to be promoted to the rank of Sergeant, there was never any question as to who should do the honors. Jackie was serving as a First Sergeant (1SG) of a field artillery unit at Fort Sill at the time, and he proudly accepted the time-honored tradition of pinning on my stripes.

At the promotion ceremony, I stood at attention, my chest swelling with a mixture of pride and hard-won triumph. On one side stood the troop commander, and on the other stood Jackie. As they stepped forward to pin the chevrons to my collar, it became one of the proudest moments of my life. Having my oldest brother—the man who had set the standard for me since I was a small boy—be the one to recognize my transition into leadership was overwhelming. In that moment, it was not just about my rank; it was about a legacy of service being passed from one brother to the next. He had shown me how to be a man of character at the kitchen table, and now he was honoring me as a leader on the parade field.

The Silent Burden

In our family, Jackie occupied a unique position: he was the only person left with a firsthand memory of our first sibling. To the rest of us, Ronnie was a name, a photograph, or a hushed story; to Jackie, he was a brother whose laughter and presence were once tangible facts. I have often reflected on the silent, invisible weight of that inheritance. It is a heavy thing to be the sole custodian of a person's existence within a family that is trying, and failing, to move on.

Jackie was thrust into the role of the new "eldest," a position he had to navigate in a home permanently dimmed by the suffocating grief of two broken parents. He came of age in the wreckage of their loss—

one parent paralyzed by sorrow, the other a "falling-down drunk." While the rest of us were spared the direct memory of what was lost, Jackie lived in the gap between the "before" and the "after." He occupied a haunted space of recollection that we never had to enter, seeing the daily contrast between the family they were and the remnants they became.

Yet the most remarkable thing about Jackie was not the burden he carried, but how he chose to carry it. He never allowed that heavy history to harden his heart or sour his spirit. In an environment that could have easily bred resentment or despair, he made a conscious, quiet rebellion against his circumstances. He refused the easy path of the martyr. Instead of becoming a victim of his family's ghosts, he chose to be a builder—constructing a life of purpose out of the very bricks that had once felt too heavy to lift.

Full Speed Ahead

Mike was the next in our family's line of service. Like Jackie before him, he donned the uniform of the United States Army, and during my early, formative years, he was stationed at Fort Sill. I carry a vivid, indelible memory of him coming over for lunch one day; to my young eyes, he looked like a giant. He stood tall in his crisp, starched fatigues and polished boots, which captured the light.

On that day, he sat me down and spent most of his lunch teaching me how to tie my shoes. It is a small, simple memory, but it represents something much larger: it was one of the many ways my siblings stepped into the gaps to parent me when my father, consumed by his own battles, simply could not.

Mike was the person who first introduced me to the power of music, providing a safe harbor during a time when there were precious few other outlets for joy or escape. He owned a massive collection of vinyl albums—vast, heavy cases of treasures from the 60s and 70s that became my literal portal to another world.

I would get lost in those records for hours on end, mesmerized by the art on the jackets and the magic hidden in the grooves. Even now, if I close my eyes and reminisce, I can still recall the scent of that room—a distinct, nostalgic cocktail of pressed vinyl, settling dust, and the sharp, chemical tang of record cleaner.

A Rock and Roll Education

By the time I was eight years old, I had received an education in rock and roll second to none. While other kids were listening to nursery rhymes or children's records, I was a student of the greats. I knew more about Foghat, Savoy Brown, Nazareth, Foreigner, and Journey than any other child before or since.

Music became the chronological map of my life. Every significant event, every struggle, and every triumph seems to have a specific song etched into the memory alongside it. These tracks are more than just background noise; they are time machines. To this day, when I hear those familiar opening chords, I am transported instantly back to those moments—the good, the bad, and everything in between—feeling the same emotions as if I were eight years old all over again.

More importantly, I learned that music was a fortress. It was a way to tune out the screaming and yelling that permeated our house. It allowed me to get away mentally when I could not leave physically, and it gave me a language to express the emotions I did not yet have words for. This made such a profound impact on me that music became my first professional calling. As a teenager, I would "officially and unofficially" DJ my friends' parties, which led to a career working at radio stations and teen clubs in Texas and Oklahoma before I finally followed my brothers' path into the Army.

I also carry a cherished memory of one Christmas that felt like a movie scene. Mike arrived at the house with his heavy, olive-drab military laundry bag slung over his shoulder. He looked like a part-time military Santa Claus, with a bag that was overflowing with gifts for all of us. In a house where "extra" was a rare word, that laundry bag felt like a miracle.

Beyond the music and the gifts, Mike set a standard for our family. He was the first among us to graduate from college—a feat he achieved not through luck or privilege, but through sheer, unadulterated persistence. He worked long, grueling hours, balancing life's demands with his studies, and he simply refused to quit. From him, I learned a lesson that would later serve me well in the desert and on the streets: your starting point never has to dictate your finish line.

The Second Mom

Darlene, who is ten years my senior, occupied a space in my life that was far more significant than that of a sister; she was a second mother. From the very moment I was brought home from the hospital, she claimed me as her own, and my earliest perspective of the world was often from the vantage point of being perched firmly on her hip. That bond, forged in those quiet, foundational years of her carrying me through our house, has remained ironclad. It is a connection that has never frayed, regardless of the miles or the decades that have passed since.

Throughout my life, Darlene has served as my steady pillar of support. When the currents of life were at their most turbulent, and I found myself at my lowest points, she was the one who remained unmoved. She never offered the cold sting of judgment or the weight of condemnation; instead, she always extended a hand to lift me back up, offering the kind of grace that only someone who truly knows your heart can provide.

Darlene and her husband Phil—known affectionately as Uncle Phil —have been a constant source of provision and wisdom in my life. Phil was the perennial child at heart and a relentless prankster; he lived for the moment he could catch us off guard and give us a good scare.

When he successfully scared someone or found something particularly hilarious, he would let out a staccato burst of high-pitched laughter—a sound so infectious that it made everyone around him join in. He had a unique way of speaking, too; he called everyone "Asso" affectionately. While it sounded like a variation of a curse word, we all knew it was strictly a term of endearment in Phil's vocabulary.

Heaven forbid I should call him the day after his birthday! He would pick up the phone and immediately shout, "You forgot, Asso!" before breaking into that signature high-pitched laugh that only he could produce. It was impossible not to laugh along with him.

I will never forget his specific quirks, which were as much a part of him as his sense of humor. He had a deep, unwavering love for chocolate almond ice cream, and I can still see the methodical way he would use his pointer finger to break his potato chips into smaller, bite-sized pieces before eating them.

As soon as he clocked off work, his routine was set - he'd be in his shorts, barefoot, meticulously taking care of the lawn. He found joy in the simple labor of maintaining his home, and that same care extended to us. Phil did not just tend to the grass; he tended to our hearts. He and Darlene did not just exist on the periphery of my story; they were woven into my life continually. Whether it was through their time, resources, or unwavering belief in me, they invested in my future with selfless consistency. I am forever grateful for the harvest of character they helped cultivate within me—a harvest nurtured by their living example of what a strong, loving marriage and a dedicated family should look like.

Beyond the deep emotional support, Darlene was the curator of my childhood joys. I remember vividly how she would always be the one to cut my hair, transforming her kitchen into a makeshift barbershop. In those days, I had a specific vision for my style; I was determined to look exactly like Rick Springfield. Darlene would patiently work with the shears, navigating my cowlicks to try and match that iconic 1980s look, treating my childhood vanity with the utmost care.

She and Phil were also the architects of our greatest summer adventures. Every year, like clockwork, they would load us up and take us to Six Flags. Those trips were more than just days at an amusement park; they were a necessary reprieve from the daily grind and a rare chance to simply be kids. We created memories filled with adrenaline and laughter that I still hold dear today. If I close my eyes, I can still smell the sunbaked blacktop of the park and taste the legendary "Pink Thing" frozen treats they used to sell.

Darlene provided the fun, the fashion, and the foundation. She showed me that love is often found in the small, consistent acts—a haircut, a road trip, or a firm hand to hold. I am the man I am today because of the hip she carried me on all those years ago. Darlene and Phil spent their lives watering my soul, and the fruit of their labor is evident in every gap I stand in today.

The Breath of Fresh Air

Mary is the next vital link in the family lineage, and she has always been what we fondly call a "nut"—in the most loving, life-giving sense of the word. In a house where our father's addiction often created a heavy, suffocating atmosphere that felt like it was pressing the air out of the room, Mary was the oxygen. Her laughter was infectious, and her constant, radiant smile served as a stark, necessary contrast to the shadows that dwelled in the corners of our home.

But I have learned over the years: do not let that bright, cheerful exterior fool you for a second—the woman is dangerous! Mary has a very specific, refined set of skills that could make a seasoned soldier flinch. She mastered the art of "toe-pinching," a stealthy maneuver where she could pinch the absolute fire out of us using nothing but her toes. It was a tactical strike you never saw coming, and it usually left us howling while she went right back to that innocent smile.

Beyond her humor and her "deadly" toes, Mary's love for pickles and snacks is nothing short of legendary. It was not just a preference; it was a lifestyle. To this day, the tradition is still unchanged. A trip to Mary's house is a guarantee of many things—warmth, laughter, and the absolute certainty that pickles will be served to everyone in attendance. It is her signature, a small but consistent comfort that says you are home.

On a much deeper level, Mary and her husband, David, have been a bedrock of support for me. Life has not always been a straight path; I had my "lost and found" years—seasons when I wandered, struggled, and fought to find my way back to the man I was meant to be. Through every high and every gut-wrenching low, Mary and David stood by me with a loyalty that never wavered, a testament to the kind of unconditional love that anchors a soul.

They did not just watch from the sidelines as I navigated those storms; they stayed firmly in my corner, offering a steady, quiet presence that reminded me I was still part of the unit. Their home was always a safe harbor when the world felt cold, and their support was a bridge that carried me from who I once was to the man I am today.

This support became literal and lifesaving after I was involved in a serious accident. During my recovery, when I was at my most vulnerable, they opened their home and allowed me to stay with them to recuperate. They did this while simultaneously raising their own three children—Misty, Leslie, and David Jr. Rather than me being a burden to the household, I found that their children took a keen, compassionate interest in my recovery, helping me get back on my feet in both big and small ways. For their kindness and for the way that entire family rallied around me, I am eternally grateful.

In the complex geography of our family, where the terrain can sometimes be rugged and the paths unclear, Mary has always been the light that refused to go out. Mary and David never lost heart in me, and the "due season" of my life is a direct result of the seeds of grace they planted during my darkest hours.

The Professor

Next in line was Joe, who occupied that volatile middle ground of childhood. He was just old enough to lead our band of misfits, yet just young enough to land us all in deep water. Joe was the undisputed "idea man" of our trio—a thinker who often devised unique ways to have fun, though his plans usually culminated in a physics experiment that went spectacularly, and often loudly, wrong.

Even at the summer camp we attended, Joe's reputation preceded him. The counselors and kids called him "The Professor" because of his idiosyncratic way of studying insects and rocks, giving each of them unique, scientific-sounding names. But Joe was not just a scholar; he was a sharpshooter. He was known neighborhood-wide for his rock-throwing prowess and his uncanny ability to shoot our battered, weary Daisy BB gun.

The rifle was a wreck—it had a bent front sight and a dented barrel—but we spent countless hours in the dirt mastering it. We learned to shoot with surgical precision, mentally compensating for the warped barrel and the crooked sight until we could pick matchsticks out of the ground from a distance.

The Great Spray Paint Incident

I will never forget the time Joe found a stash of old spray-paint cans. He began shaking them, listening intently to the rattling of the mixing ball inside. On the spot, he decided he was going to extract that marble. Using an old Army folding shovel, he took a stance and stabbed the can with all his might.

There was a deafening **POP**. When the yellow mist finally cleared, Joe was standing there, frozen, completely coated from head to toe in a dull yellow paint. Mom had to drag him inside to scrub the pigment from his face and eyes while he looked at me with a sheepish, yellow-tinted grin. To this day, I still do not know if he ever actually got that marble.

As Joe grew older, his love of the Lord grew exponentially, and he consistently followed his heart toward the things of God. He spent many nights walking to church on Wednesdays—a solitary but determined figure—even when everyone else was home watching television or playing sports. I watched his Christian walk mature over the years, and I can honestly say that his steadfast example helped me through seasons when I was lost, confused, and living for myself. Joe was always ready to pray with us, acting as a spiritual leader and helping us hold on to our faith when the grip of the world felt too strong.

His wife, Karen, is another indispensable part of my story. She is solidly and unapologetically "stuck in the '70s," keeping a style and spirit that brings a unique warmth to our lives. Karen has been a constant friend and a faithful companion through countless life events, standing by us through every twist and turn. Her sense of humor is a treasure, and the classic, regional way she says "warsh rag" is a quirk that will never get old.

Together, Joe and Karen represent a legacy of consistency. In a world that is always changing, their presence provides a sense of continuity and peace. Joe lived that out on those Wednesday night walks. He stirred up the faith in me just by showing up, and Karen's joy served as the perfect complement to his devotion.

The Shield

Billy was the next oldest and the closest in age to me. For much of my youth, he played a dual role: he was the source of my growing pains and my ultimate defender. Because we were so close in age, we spent much of our time together, side by side, forging a bond that grew deeper than any other over the decades. He was not just a brother; he was the shadow that walked beside me, often leading the way through the thicket.

We were tough kids from a tough neighborhood, raised in a world where vulnerability was a liability. In our circle, showing any kind of "softness" was seen as a tactical error—an invitation for ridicule or laughter from the very people you called friends. We were trained by our environment to be rugged, and so, we never really learned the vocabulary to express our emotions. We did not talk about our feelings; we just lived them out.

In the quiet, unspoken spaces of my heart, however, I always knew I could count on Billy's strength. He acted as a living shield for me, standing in the gap against threats and hardships I do not even know about to this day. Billy was a protector at his very core—it was a part of his DNA. Behind the scenes, he pulled me out of more messes than I can count, often covering for me before I even realized I was in trouble.

His loyalty was absolute and fierce. While we might have had our share of brotherly scraps—the kind of roughhousing that happens when two young boys are testing their limits—the second an outside threat appeared, the internal fight was over. He was the first person to step in if anyone else dared to lay a finger on me. He took his role as the older brother seriously, providing a perimeter of safety that allowed me to grow. Billy was born for the adversity of our youth, ensuring that no matter how rough the neighborhood got, the caboose was never left behind or unprotected.

· · ·

The Underdog Bites Back

Being two years older, Billy took his role as big brother seriously. In the hierarchy of our backyard, that usually meant I was his favorite to pick on. One afternoon, after Billy and his friends had given me a particularly thorough walloping—the kind that left you dusty, stinging, and humiliated—I decided that enough was enough. In the way only a slighted younger brother can, I decided he needed to be taught a lesson.

I grabbed that old, weary Daisy BB gun—bent sight, dented barrel, and all—and took aim. As Billy sauntered across the street, his head held high with the confidence of his recent victory, I let loose.

THWACK! The copper-plated BB found its mark, hitting him squarely in the leg of his Wranglers. In our house, all clothes were second or third-hand hand-me-downs, and Billy's jeans were no exception. They were about two sizes too small and skin-tight, leaving zero denim buffer between the BB and his hide. He yelped in pure surprise, fire igniting in his eyes as he spun around and began charging toward me.

THWACK. THWACK. THWACK. I did not flinch. I kept a steady rate of fire, pumping BB's until he was rolling on the ground. He suddenly realized that I had a full magazine and a clear line of sight. It was a moment of sweet, localized revenge—the underdog finally biting back. But the victory was short-lived. Just as I was preparing for another volley, a firm, unmistakable hand clamped down on the barrel of the gun.

Mom.

The aftermath was swift. I received a vivid, memorable spanking while Billy—nursing his pride and his stinging legs—grinned triumphantly from the safety of the next room. I knew I deserved the discipline, and a part of me felt bad about it later, but for that one fleeting moment in the street, the underdog had held his ground. I had learned that even when you are outmatched, a well-placed shot and a bit of resolve can change the entire battlefield.

Billy (now known to us as Bill) and his wife, Pam, remain steadfast in their mission to protect and care for others. They have dedicated their lives to the quiet, essential work of the Kingdom, serving veterans who have sacrificed for our country and watching over children with a tenderness that reflects the heart of the Father.

While they walk out their calling, they continue doing exactly what God has asked them to do: **serve.** They are the hands and feet of Christ, often operating entirely behind the scenes, pouring out love and care upon people who may never even know the names of those who blessed them. They do not seek the spotlight or the credit; they find their fulfillment in the act of obedience and the joy of seeing someone else's burden lifted.

Bill and Pam understand that true impact is not measured by applause, but by the legacy of love left in the lives of the "least of these." Their consistency in service gives a beautiful example of what it means to be a servant in the quiet, everyday spaces of life.

3

THE ANCHOR AND THE GHOST

Our lives were built on a foundation of faith that my mother laid, brick by brick, in the unforgiving red Oklahoma dirt. That dirt—stained the color of rust and dried blood—clung to everything we owned, a constant reminder of the earth we came from. But for as long as I can remember, we were not defined by the dirt; the Church defined us. It was not a social club where people went to see and be seen; it was a lifeline thrown to a drowning family.

Our faith was not a "Sunday-best" garment to be taken out and pressed once a week. It was woven into the second and third-hand clothes we wore every day to survive. It was in the frayed collars and the hand-me-down shoes. Even when our tired, rusted car would not start—which was often—my mother would not let that be an excuse for spiritual laziness. When the engine gave that final, pathetic click of a dead battery, she did not collapse in defeat. Instead, she would gather us up, slick our hair down with Brylcreem until it shone, and lead us out the door. We would walk the miles to church, a small procession of poverty-stricken pilgrims marching through the heat.

She walked with a quiet, stubborn dignity that told the world our circumstances did not define our worth. I can still hear her shoes on

23

the pavement—a steady sound that signaled her unbreakable resolve. To her, the church was not just a building with pews and a pulpit; it was the only place where the specter of poverty could not follow us. Inside those walls, the drafty house, the empty cupboards, and the judgmental whispers of the town faded away. Inside, we were not the "poor family"; we were children of the King, royalty in a kingdom that did not use money as its currency.

The Shadow of 1957

While my mother was our spiritual anchor, my father was a ghost, haunted by a boy I never knew. My oldest brother, Ronnie, had left this world at just five years old in 1957, a full decade before I was even a thought. It was a tragedy involving a botched "routine" tonsillectomy that went horribly wrong.

The hospital had sent him home while his blood refused to clot. My father had to hold his son as he bled, the small boy's life spilling out in a warm, terrifying rush onto his clothes, his hands, and his heart. He had to listen to Ronnie plead, "It hurts, please make it stop, Daddy," and he could not. He was a father, the protector of the home, and he was forced to stand by as death took his son in the most gut-wrenching way imaginable.

That moment did not just hurt my father; it shattered something fundamental in his soul. The "falling down drunk" was the only way he knew how to drown out that high, thin voice crying for help he could not provide. The haunting memory kept my dad prisoner, which in turn kept us at arm's length from homelessness. His search for peace in a bottle kept us prisoners of poverty for years to come.

He was physically present in our home, but his heart was often stuck in 1957, still trying to stop the bleeding. He was not a "functioning alcoholic" who could keep the charade of a steady job. Once he took a single drink, the slide began. He would drink until the world went dark, until he did not have to think or function as an adult.

This trauma spilled out into our most public moments. There were more times than I can count when he would show up at our little-league games, swaying on the sidelines, smelling of cheap beer, and becoming belligerent with parents and umpires. The embarrassment was a heavy weight. I remember the times he would wet himself in public or grow violent with anyone who tried to take his beer. We tried everything—hiding the cans, pouring the liquor down the drain—but it usually ended in a terrifying rage.

The Long Road to Fort Supply

Whenever the darkness of my father's addiction became too deep to navigate, there was only one path back to the light: getting him to the state hospital in Fort Supply, Oklahoma. It was a place of temporary refuge, a facility where he would remain sequestered until he was sober and clean, usually for a couple of weeks. But the journey to those hospital gates was a mission that required a deceptive, agonizing strategy.

Because his admission was entirely voluntary, we were trapped in a fragile game of compliance. Between the two of them, Jackie and Mom had to orchestrate a way to lure him into the car using the very catalyst of his destruction—beer. They had to drive him across the state, maintaining a steady supply of alcohol just to keep him from turning back or becoming combative.

The process was a grueling, emotional gauntlet. They had to ensure he had all he wanted to drink, keeping him in a state of blurred cooperation just long enough to reach the facility and convince him to sign the papers. To see my mother and my brother forced into the role of enablers—feeding the addiction specifically to reach the cure—was a trauma all its own. They were navigating a razor's edge, praying the "bait" would last until the car crossed into the hospital grounds. Once inside, the cycle would pause. Fort Supply became the place where the man we knew could finally emerge from the fog of the "falling-down drunk" he had become. He would stay there until the toxins cleared and he was deemed fit to return home, but the cost of getting him there was a debt the family paid in spirit. We were stuck in a loop of heartbreak, using the bottle to buy his freedom from it again and again.

With our family living on the razor's edge of poverty, those long trips to Fort Supply would have been an impossible luxury to manage on our own. Our finances were often as depleted as our spirits, making the cost of gas and the wear on our vehicle a hurdle we could not clear without help. It was the selfless intervention of my older siblings—each stepping up at one point or another—that made the journey practical. They provided the means when we were without and the strength when our own internal resources had run dry, acting as the bridge that allowed us to cross the state toward Dad's recovery.

I cannot count how many times during my youth we made that long, somber, four-hour trek across the Oklahoma landscape. The scenery of those drives is burned into my memory: the flat, red-dirt horizon stretching out endlessly, punctuated by the rhythmic hum of tires on the pavement and the heavy silence within the car.

Every mile was a testament to our family's fortitude. We were a unit operating on a cycle of crisis and rescue, and while the destination was always a hospital, the journey itself was a grueling exercise in loyalty. My siblings did not just hand over money; they handed over their time and their peace of mind, ensuring that, even when the train sputtered, it never quite ran off the tracks. We were poor in pocket, but in those moments of crossing the plains, we were rich in the kind of fierce, protective love that only a family can generate.

The Sunday Run

I remember one specific trip to Fort Supply that stands out from the rest. I was only eight years old, tucked into the car with Jackie, Debbie, and Mom. We had set out in the quiet chill of a Sunday morning, a timing necessitated by the rigid demands of the working world; Jackie had to be back at work the following morning, leaving us no room for delay or error.

The first leg of the journey was a success in the most clinical sense. We navigated the miles to Fort Supply without incident, successfully managed the delicate task of getting Dad through the hospital doors, and watched as he signed himself in. With that mission accomplished, we immediately turned the car around to begin the long trek back across the Oklahoma plains.

However, the relief of the successful drop-off was quickly overshadowed by the reality of our own depletion. By the time we began the return journey, we were entirely out of food and water. Whatever meager rations we had managed to pack for the four-hour drive up had been finished, leaving us with nothing but empty containers and the gnawing hunger. We were a car full of people who had just navigated a major family trauma, now facing a half-day's journey home on empty stomachs and parched throats.

The adrenaline of the mission was gone, replaced by a weary, hollow exhaustion as we watched the sun begin to shift over a landscape that offered no easy comforts.

About ten minutes after leaving the facility, the car began smoking and sputtering. Jackie had no choice but to pull over onto the shoulder of a desolate, shimmering highway. There we were—Jackie, Debbie, Mom, and me—standing on the side of a scorching Oklahoma road, hoping for a miracle. Because it was Sunday, the road was a ghost ribbon, with little to no traffic.

As the heat began to bake the asphalt, we started walking toward the next town, trying our best not to overheat. Mom held my hand firmly. She looked down at me and said, "We are okay. God always takes care of us; just never forget to pray for His help." So, in the simplicity of an eight-year-old's heart, I did what I knew how to do: I prayed.

Before you knew it, an RV appeared on the horizon. It passed us, then slowed and came to a halt. A woman in her mid-forties stepped out and waved us toward her with a curious, kind gaze. We hurried along the side of the road to catch up. A man—her husband—and a young teenage girl joined her. While Jackie spoke to the man, the woman and the girl ushered Mom, Debbie, and me into the cool interior of the RV, immediately providing us with water and snacks.

Jackie soon joined us inside as the couple climbed into the front seats and drove us back toward our stricken car. Jackie leaned over and whispered, "This couple owns a gas station. They've offered to go get parts from their shop and fix the car for us." I looked at Mom and smiled, the quiet realization washing over me that God had once again taken care of us, just as she said He would.

The couple took us to their home, where we were invited to relax. We sat and talked openly about our mission to Fort Supply, sharing the burden we were carrying. While the wife stayed with us, Jackie and the husband drove to the gas station, gathered the necessary parts, and returned to the highway to repair our vehicle.

Once the car was running, Jackie followed the man to his station while his wife drove the rest of us there to meet him. They went above and beyond, insisting on filling our tank with gas and packing us a bag of drinks and snacks for the remainder of the trip to Lawton. I remember seeing Jackie reach into his pocket and offer the man a twenty-dollar bill—literally all the money we had at the time. The man simply shook his head and said, "No, we want to bless you."

Before we left, the teenage girl reached for one of the air fresheners they sold at the station and handed it to me. It was a little poodle made of pipe cleaners that smelled like vanilla. I never did learn their names, but that family blessed us more than they could ever imagine.

On that scorching Sunday, on a road that felt abandoned by everyone else, those "angels" in an RV taught me that when you are on God's assignment—even a painful one like delivering a father to rehab—He provides the service.

Each trip we made was a lesson in the high cost of "holding it together." It was a relentless monster, an insatiable void that demanded to be filled. When beer or liquor were unavailable, his desperation drove him to consume mouthwash or any household product with an alcohol content.

I vividly remember the chaos of the day he drank an old bottle of cologne. His body, unable to process the perfumes and toxic chemicals, gave out entirely; he collapsed on the floor, unconscious and unresponsive. The scene ended with the sterile glare of an ambulance and the sight of him being carted away to the hospital.

Living with him meant navigating a volatile cycle—watching my dad shift from a passed-out stupor to a state of raging anger. This constant instability shattered any sense of youthful peace, forcing me to remain on guard at all times.

To Dial or not to Dial

One memory stands out with the clarity of a nightmare. I was only six years old. Mom reached her breaking point and tried to take his bottle of liquor away. The air in the house changed instantly. Things got violent. He started fighting with her, his movements erratic and fueled by a desperate need for the bottle, and he managed to get his arm around her neck.

I ran to the kitchen, my heart pounding in my ears. At school, they had recently taught us how to dial 911 in emergencies. I held the heavy plastic receiver to my ear, my finger hovering over the dial, debating whether to call the police on my own father. As I watched my mom struggle, her face changing color as she started choking, she bit his arm in a desperate act of self-defense. I saw the blood start to flow from the bite.

I heard a hollow, distant voice speaking into the phone: "Can you send the police? My dad is hurting my mom." It took me a second to realize the voice was mine. I sat there, small and trembling, and watched as the police arrived. I watched them lead my father away in handcuffs, his head hanging, and I wondered what I had done. I loved my dad, but I did not know my dad. I only knew his actions and the wreckage they left behind.

The Seesaw of Survival

When the shadows of 1957 retreated long enough for him to find his footing, my father was a man of remarkable industry. In those windows of sobriety, he was not just a "painter"—he was a craftsman. He had a level of skill that was respected across the city. He would be up before the first hint of orange broke over the Oklahoma horizon, the smell of strong black coffee and turpentine trailing behind him. He worked grueling, back-breaking hours, climbing ladders under the blistering sun and painting houses until the dusk settled into the trees.

He was skilled, he made decent money, and in those good months, he was never short on work. The community knew that if you wanted a job done right, you called him. During these times, the house felt different. There was a sense of stability, a fleeting hope that, just maybe, this time the peace would stick.

Dad's love for the outdoors was our primary connection to him. He loved fishing and hunting, and when he was sober, these were not just hobbies; they were a means of providing for his family. He would proudly bring home new shotguns and sturdy fishing poles. We all grew up with the rugged education of the field. We learned how to clean fish by the glow of a porch light and how to dress rabbits, squirrels, and doves after a successful outing. There was a primal sort of pride in sitting down to a meal that he had provided with his own two hands.

It was not just the meat on the table, either. In the flush of a steady paycheck, he would bring home the "extras" that made us feel like a normal family. He would buy a television—the glowing centerpiece of our living room—and baseball bats for us to take to the empty field across the street. He would replenish the heavy, steel tools of his trade, ensuring he had the best brushes and scrapers to keep the money coming in.

But we lived in a house where the floorboards held their breath. We grew to hate the "coming home" moment. It was the daily gamble of every alcoholic's child. We would walk through the door after school, praying for the silence of a house where Mom was cooking and Dad was washing the paint off his hands. Instead, we would often be met with a different kind of silence—or worse, the heavy, drunken snoring of a man defeated.

We would find him passed out, the air thick and reeking of stale beer and urine. The shift was palpable. The man who had been a provider just days before would vanish, replaced by a desperate stranger. Then began the "inventory of loss." To feed the next bottle, he would strip our lives of their luster. He would take everything—the bats we used for practice, the tools he needed to earn a living, the TV we gathered around, and even the guns and fishing poles that had put food on our table.

He would haul them all to the local pawn shop, trading our childhood joys and his own professional future for the meager handful of cash needed for the next drink. Each trip to the pawn shop was a brick removed from the foundation of our security.

Government Grace

I had no idea then about the demons he was fighting. I did not see the ghost of my five-year-old brother, Ronnie; I did not see the five-year-old boy bleeding out in 1957. I was too young to understand that he was not drinking away our furniture—he was trying to drink away a memory that was eating him alive. At the time, I only saw the empty spot on the broken television console where the new TV had been. I only knew that we did not have what we needed.

Because of the bottle's cycle, we lived on the government's grace. Living on the south side of town, we attended Lincoln Elementary School, which holds the distinction of being the oldest school building still standing in Lawton. In those days, the morning routine was a public ritual that defined your social standing before the first bell had even finished ringing. The teacher would call out the roll, and as each name was read, you were expected to walk your lunch money up to the teacher's desk. In my case—as it was for those of us whose families struggled to make ends meet—when my name was called, I was expected to call out "free," announcing that we did not have to pay for lunch. On one specific morning in the 1st grade. I happened to have fifteen cents in my pocket, and to me, that felt like a fortune. When the teacher called my name, instead of staying in my seat and uttering that familiar, humbling word, I stood up. I walked toward the front of the room with my head held high, intending to pay for my lunch simply because, for once, I could.

I reached the desk and proudly placed my fifteen cents down. I wanted to feel like everyone else; I wanted to be a contributor rather than a recipient. However, the teacher looked at me with a mix of surprise and confusion that quickly chilled my spirit. Rather than a quiet "thank you," she spoke loudly enough for the entire room to hear.

"Please take your change," she said. "You should know you don't have to pay for your lunch because your family can't afford it. Save that and help your family."

In an instant, my sense of pride was crushed into a heavy, suffocating shame. I felt my face turn beet red as the sound of the class laughing filled my ears. A few cents, which had felt like a badge of honor in my pocket, suddenly felt like a brand of poverty on my palm.

That day at Lincoln Elementary, my spirit felt the weight of a world that judges by the purse rather than the heart. It was a lesson in the sting of public humiliation, but it also planted a seed in me—a drive to one day reach a place where I could not only pay my own way but provide for others who stood exactly where I was standing. It was not all bad at Lincoln Elementary, though. While the sting of earlier years lingered, the atmosphere shifted a few years later when a teacher truly spoke life into me. She saw past the "free lunch" label and recognized the potential hidden beneath the surface, encouraging me to believe I could be so much more than my circumstances suggested.

I was in the fifth grade when a new teacher, Donna Kriz, came to Lincoln. From the moment she arrived, she stood out. She was so kind and loving; you just knew, without a doubt, that she was a genuine person who cared deeply for her "kids." She did not just teach curriculum; she nurtured souls.

One day after school, when the hallways had grown quiet, she stopped me. She looked me square in the eye—with a sincerity that demanded I pay attention—and said, **"You are an amazing young man, and one day you will do amazing things."**

In that moment, the shame of the fifteen cents and the laughter of the classroom seemed to lose their power. Her words acted as a prophetic shield, protecting the "amazing young man" she saw from the doubts I had about myself. I carried that sentence with me for the rest of my life. It became a mantle I reached for during the grueling days of basic training, the terrifying nights in the Iraqi desert, and the high-pressure shifts on the police force.

Donna Kriz poured that sweetness into my soul when I needed it most, proving that a single sentence from a person who cares can change the entire trajectory of a child's life. She planted a seed of greatness in me that I have spent the rest of my years trying to harvest for the glory of God.

· · ·

Paper Money

I remember the food stamps vividly. While other kids in more affluent parts of town might have been embarrassed to see those booklets come out, to us, they were a cause for celebration. We were ecstatic for grocery day. In those days, food stamps were not plastic cards; they were like colorful paper dollar bills in different denominations.

To a child, they looked like play money, but they stood for the only real security we had. Mom, in her infinite grace, would occasionally give us a dollar in food stamps and let us pick out candy. In those moments, clutching a blue or orange slip of paper that would buy us a pack of gum or a chocolate bar, we thought we were rich.

It was not until much later, looking back through the eyes of an adult, that I recognized the tragedy in those scenes. I can now see the specific look in the cashiers' eyes as they watched two young boys pay for candy with a food stamp dollar—a mixture of pity, concern, and a quiet, weary kind of care. They saw our cheap, uneven haircuts and the second-hand clothes, and knew the story we did not understand and were too young to tell.

The Silver and Gold of Commodities

During the leanest stretches of my childhood, our pantry was supplemented by the government. On certain designated days, the state handed out food in the form of government commodities—staples that arrived in utilitarian silver cans stripped of any vibrant branding, marked only with plain black lettering. While much of those rations have faded from my memory, two items remain etched in my mind with startling clarity: the meat and the cheese.

"Dog Meat" and Silver Cans

The meat was a mystery in a tin. We affectionately, if somewhat irreverently, called it "dog meat" because of its unappealing appearance; once it was sliced and released from the can, it bore a striking resemblance to wet dog food. Looking back through the lens of adulthood, I suspect it was either SPAM or a generic, industrial-grade replica. Despite its nickname and its questionable aesthetic, it was a staple that filled our bellies when other options were scarce.

The Golden Block

In stark contrast to the "dog meat," the cheese was a prized treasure. It arrived in a long, narrow cardboard box—a sturdy brick of processed gold that we could not wait to tear into. There was something celebratory about opening that box. We would carefully slice thick slabs of it to layer onto crackers or press between slices of bread to make grilled cheese sandwiches. Unlike the mystery meat, the cheese was genuinely good, melting into a creamy, comforting consistency that felt like a luxury in a house that had seen so many "hard winters."

Those silver cans and cardboard boxes were more than just food; they were the tangible markers of our survival, the government-issued fuel that kept the "caboose" and the rest of the train moving forward.

Provision

We were provided for in some very trying times, even if it was not the way we would have chosen. We were fed because of those food stamps, government commodities, and the fortitude of our mother. Looking back, I cannot fathom the sheer weight my mother carried. She was the one who had to manage the shame of the pawn shop, the volatility of a drunk husband, and the hungry eyes of her children.

She did her absolute best to provide us with the basics, keeping her head held high while her husband was miles away, mentally and emotionally lost in a hospital room in 1957, still trying to stop the bleeding that had never truly ended. Her strength was the bridge between our poverty and our potential, and she never let that bridge break.

4

OUR HOUSE

The house we lived in was not so much a shelter as it was a sieve for the elements. It sat on the edge of Lawton, a collection of wood and prayer that seemed to lean away from the north wind. We were cold in the winter and stifled in the summer. We had old gas heaters that hissed like snakes and a swamp cooler that did little more than blow the humid heat around in scorching Oklahoma summers.

In winter, the struggle for warmth was a daily ritual. We would light the old gas heaters, the blue flames casting dancing shadows on the walls, and Mom would stuff towels or old blankets around the windows to stop the whistling drafts. There were no seals on those windows, and when the temperature plummeted, ice would form on the inside of the glass. I used to scratch my name into the frost, marveling at how the world outside was frozen so hard it had forced its way into our living room.

Our floors were wood and covered by linoleum that was torn and worn thin in areas, a roadmap of where we walked the most. We would walk on the bare wood in some places and get splinters if we were not careful. The walls were a patchwork of damage—dents from moving furniture, scratches from kids playing, and the general wear and tear of a large family in a small space. The kitchen wall where the phone hung served as our community directory. It was covered in phone numbers written by adults and teenagers in pencil or pen for quick access—doctors, relatives, and employers scrawled directly onto the exposed sheetrock.

The Kitchen

The kitchen was the heart of our struggle, yet it was also the center of our survival. Our refrigerator was a vivid, chaotic mosaic of stickers, a collection of small prizes won at carnivals or discovered hidden inside packages of gum. It was a relic of another era—so old that the handle had long since broken off. I remember the specific ritual of opening it: we had to wedge our fingers deep into the yellowing rubber seal in the crack of the door and pull with all our might just to break the vacuum.

The kitchen did not have cabinets for dishes and cups. Instead, there were a couple of shelves fashioned over the sink. We did not own china or fine glasses; we had plastic plates and red plastic cups like the ones you see in diners that had survived a thousand drops. Our bowls were old butter containers that were repurposed and scrubbed clean. Our pantry was a floor-to-ceiling set of shelves with a board halfway up used as a countertop. It sat fixed next to an old gas model stove that, in darkness, would cast an eerie, constant glow from the pilot lights on the burners. There was a table in the kitchen and six chairs, each of a different origin and design—one metal, one wood, one with a cracked vinyl seat. It was a tight fit for a family of our size, but being the youngest, I could squirm my way anywhere. I spent a sizable part of my childhood playing underneath that table. It was my fort, my bunker, and a safe refuge for me when I got in trouble. From under there, the world was just a forest of table legs and adult work boots.

. . .

The Constant Squatters

Mice were our constant, unwanted squatters, which explains why we always kept cats. These cats were not the pampered, cuddly indoor pets you see in catalogs; they were elite, "super-hunters" that treated our home as their personal territory. They only ventured inside with a specific purpose: to hunt what was supposed to stay outside.

The mice themselves were incredibly bold. They did not just hide in the walls; they would occasionally end up nestled inside our shoes or scurry across the pots and pans in the middle of the night, their tiny claws creating a metallic scratching sound that echoed through the dark.

Our feline guardians often insisted on sharing their victories with us. Many times, one of the cats would catch a mouse and bring the still-living trophy right to where we were sitting, forcing us to watch as they played with their prey. Other times, the evidence was grizzlier— we would wake up to find the half-eaten remains of a mouse left in the middle of the floor like a grim offering. Whether the mice were scurrying or the cats were hunting, it was never a pleasant experience; it was simply another layer of the sights and sounds that defined the landscape of my youth.

Despite our constant efforts to keep some semblance of cleanliness, I never truly grew accustomed to the sight of roaches. It was a jarring, nightly ritual: the moment you flipped the kitchen light switch, the linoleum floor would seem to ripple and move as dozens of them fled in every direction, vanishing into the cracks of the floorboards and the safety of the shadows. To a child, it was a nuisance; to an adolescent, it became a mark of "otherness."

As I grew older, the pieces of a painful puzzle began to fall into place. I started to understand why a friend from school would come over once, only to never return. I realized why the invitations were never reciprocated and why the air grew thick with an unspoken tension when a classmate stepped through our door.

When the truth finally settled in, it hit me like a physical stab in my heart. I realized that we were "those" people—the poor ones who lived in a house infested with roaches and mice. It was a crushing realization that redefined my place in the world, stripping away the innocence of my youth and replacing it with a heavy, lingering sense of shame that I had not asked for, but now had to carry.

The Threshold of Survival

Our house was never truly "shut." To use the word "closed" would imply a seal against the world that we simply did not have. The doors were old, heavy slabs of wood, warped by decades of Oklahoma humidity and bone-dry heat until they no longer fit their frames. They groaned on their hinges, and the latches rarely lined up with the strike plates. Locking them was an exercise in futility; we did not live in a house that kept things out—we lived in a house that the world breathed through.

We had screen doors on the front and back, intended to offer some semblance of a barrier against the flies and the dust. But in a house teeming with children, those screens were doomed from the start. They developed spiky, silver-rimmed holes the moment they were installed. A stray elbow, a toy flung in a moment of passion, or a foot kicking out to catch the door would leave a gap big enough for the never-ending stream of flies to fly through.

The very layout of our home served as a constant, structural reminder of our lack of resources. It was not a house designed with privacy or aesthetics in mind; it was a jigsaw puzzle of afterthoughts, a collection of rooms added on as the family grew and the money allowed.

The kitchen served as the hub of our house. Upon entering from the living room, if you kept walking in a straight line through the kitchen, you would pass directly into my parents' bedroom. Between the kitchen and their private space hung a thin, hollow door that served no real purpose other than to block out the light; it did nothing to stop the sounds of a house full of children. If you continued through their bedroom, you finally reached ours. It was a house of transit, where one life bled into the next without much of a border.

Our Room

Our sleeping quarters were defined by an old set of bunk beds that were held together by little more than prayer and ingenuity. To keep the top bunk from sliding off its posts and crashing down, someone had jammed half-pencils into the gaps between the posts to act as makeshift shims. Joe occupied the top bunk, while Billy and I shared the bottom.

Those beds were the site of our nightly tales of the wild west and treasures. I spent many nights whispering to Joe through the narrow gap between the top mattress and the wall. In the dark, we shared the secrets, fears, and ideas of three boys whose world was small, but whose imaginations were boundless.

The house itself was sagging under the weight of the years. In one corner of our bedroom ceiling, a persistent leak had slowly collected over time, creating a heavy, water-logged bulge. It drooped down toward the floor, yellow and textured, resembling a massive, prehistoric hornet's nest. We watched it with a mix of curiosity and dread, wondering when the "nest" would finally give way. My overactive imagination would take over if I woke up in the middle of the night...glancing over and half expecting it to burst and spiders to run everywhere.

The Oklahoma summers were unrelenting, turning our back bedroom into an oven. To combat the heat, Mom would turn on an old metal barracks fan we got from a military supply store. It was a heavy, dented relic that looked like it had survived a war—and sounded like it was still fighting one. When she flipped the switch, it roared to life with a mechanical drone so massive and loud that it drowned out the rest of the world.

Strangely, that chaotic noise became my inner sanctum. The rhythmic thrum of the blades lulled me into a deep sleep. It was the "deafening quietness" that I feared; if Mom slipped in to turn the fan off in the middle of the night to save electricity, I would sit bolt upright, instantly awake. My ears needed that mechanical shield to keep the silence at bay. That roar was my lullaby, at least until the Vaporizer entered my life and added its own soothing hiss to the nights.

The Vaporizer

Since I was sick often as a child, the primary medical remedy of the day was the vaporizer. It was not just a machine to me; it was the architect of my safe haven, affectionately known as "the wapie." Mom would carefully position me on the living room couch and construct an elaborate "tent" by draping a sheet over the sofa arm and a chair backed into place. The vaporizer sat tucked in the gap between the furniture, churning out a steady hiss of cool vapor. This cool, enclosed space became my safe harbor. It was within those misty, draped walls that many of my earliest experiences with the Lord were born, where I could talk to Him about anything. The white noise of the machine and the cool, heavy mist I inhaled brought me an almost instantaneous sense of comfort. I can still recall being half-asleep and feeling my mom's hand reach through the heavy folds of the tent. She would slip her hand under my shirt to rub Vicks VapoRub onto my chest. Over the years, that pungent, medicinal scent became a signal to my body that I was being cared for; it was the smell of safety.

Mom was vigilant about our recovery. She never allowed us to miss a dose of medication, often waking us in the dead of night to swallow that thick, neon-pink antibiotic. I can still recall the cloying, chalky sweetness of that liquid—a taste I certainly do not miss.

. . .

The Sounds of Closeness

Living in such a confined "jigsaw" house meant that Billy and Joe were never far away, and they never missed an opportunity to tease me. They made fun of me for my attachment to the vaporizer and how often I was in my "tent."

When you live in such close quarters, you notice the peculiar, almost biological habits of your siblings. Sickness was not just a physical state; it had a soundtrack. They knew I was down for the count when they heard the hum of the "wapie" emanating from the living room, but I had my own early warning system for them.

I knew exactly when my brothers were sick because of their distinctive, unmistakable "throwing up" sounds. Joe had an utterly unique "Brrrrrrrrrr RAH—splat" technique; he would roll his Rs with theatrical intensity before the final delivery. Billy, on the other hand, was more direct: a simple, guttural "RAHHHHHH—splat."

While this might seem like a humorous anecdote of childhood gross-out stories, for me, it was a matter of survival. Remember, I slept directly beneath and alongside my brothers. In that crowded bedroom, the "Brrrrr RAH" or the "RAHHHHH" was not just a noise —it was a flare in the night. It was the only warning I had to "beat feet" and move out of the splash zone before disaster struck. In our house, discernment started with the ears.

The Rest of the House

To get to our only bathroom, you had to perform a ritual that defied common sense: leave the warmth of the kitchen, step out the back door, and walk onto a back porch that existed in a state of perpetual incompletion. It was a gray cement slab with a skeletal wooden frame that had never been finished, a project abandoned by time or money.

Only after crossing this exposed space could you reach the bathroom door. The room was the gateway to the "back rooms," two more spaces where the older siblings lived like pioneers in their own corner of the house before eventually moving out. But the bathroom itself was a cramped, dangerous little theater of survival. Inside, packed into a footprint far too small for a family our size, were a tub, a sink, a toilet, and a small gas heater.

This heater was strategically—and precariously—placed between the toilet and the tub. On those biting Oklahoma winter days, that heater would be turned up until it roared, the metal turning white-hot and shimmering with a lethal intensity. There were no safety guards, no cages to protect small limbs. The entire unit became one giant, scalding surface. If a drop of water or a stray sleeve touched it, the metal would hiss and sizzle with a sound that signaled instant pain.

When we were small, bath time was a choreographed maneuver. Mom would have us stand on top of the closed toilet lid—the only "safe" high ground—while she rubbed us dry with a towel. She was meticulous, making sure every drop of moisture was gone so the chill of the house would not settle in our bones. But we were kids, and the heater was a source of forbidden fascination. Sometimes—actually, a lot—we would flick water from our fingertips onto the glowing metal just to watch the sizzling bubbles dance and evaporate into plumes of steam. It was a tiny, domestic magic show that invariably brought Mom's wrath down on us.

As we grew older, the toilet lid stayed the designated drying station, but the stakes grew higher as our bodies grew larger. Billy learned this the hard way. One afternoon, while drying off, he lost his footing. In a sickening blur of wet skin and hot metal, he slipped off the lid and landed right against the heater. The smell of scorched skin filled the small room as he burned the tender area under his arm. It was a scar that served as a permanent map of the house's hazards.

The bathtub offered no comfort either. It was an ancient, stained basin, and the walls surrounding it were failing. Large, black holes gaped in the plaster along the sides, exhaling drafts of chilly air that made the bathwater turn lukewarm in minutes. The floor next to the tub, where every child had stepped out with dripping feet for years, was a disaster. The linoleum had long since peeled away, exposing wood that was rotting into a soft, dark pulp. A massive hole had formed there from decades of splashing. We lived with a constant mental map of the floorboards: step here, not there. If you missed your mark, you were not just getting your feet wet; you were falling through the floor.

The back porch, that unfinished transition between the kitchen and the bathroom, was never granted the luxury of glass windows. Instead, it was a patchwork of makeshift insulation. We covered the openings in thick, translucent plastic or heavy tarps, secured with tape and hope. But the Oklahoma wind is relentless; it would catch the edges of the plastic, ripping it until the tarps flapped with a sound like gunfire in the night.

In the winter, the porch became a frozen gauntlet. When the snow drifted through the gaps in the plastic, the cement slab turned into a skating rink. You could not just "go" to the bathroom; you had to prepare for an expedition. You would have to pull on a heavy coat just to go brush your teeth, stepping over patches of ice on the floor while your breath bloomed in white clouds before you. This architectural flaw dictated our lives. It made the house a living thing—drafty, shivering in the winter, and suffocatingly hot in the summer. It was miserable, but we did not know any different. To us, this was just what "home" felt like.

5

GROWING UP

In our neighborhood, "playing" was not a structured activity with plastic toys; it meant using the raw materials God provided: dirt, mud, sharp rocks, and whatever broken glass we could scavenge from the alleys. One hot afternoon, Joe had what he considered a "brilliant" idea to test our mettle and prepare us for the hardships of life. He gathered Billy and me and marched us to the back of the yard, while he took up a position by the house. He laid out the rules of the engagement: he would throw rocks or debris at us, and if we did not move or flinch, we would be proven "brave"—just like the legendary soldiers under fire who refused to blink in the face of the enemy.

Being the youngest, the smallest, and undoubtedly the most gullible member of the squad, I stood there like a stone statue, determined to be a hero in the eyes of my older brothers. Rocks and any other objects he could find whizzed past my head, thudding into the dirt around my feet, but I did not budge. I was a "soldier" in training, holding the line. Then, Joe threw a sharp, broken piece of glass. It did not whiz past; it caught the top of my shoulder, slicing through my thin shirt and deep into the skin.

At first, I did not feel the pain, just the impact. But then I saw the dark red stain spreading across my sleeve, a visceral mark of the "battle." In an instant, my hero act crumbled into tears. Joe turned as white as a sheet, his face a mask of pure terror. He was not sure if he had killed me or if Mom was going to finish the job once she saw the damage. He had to think fast—a true battlefield promotion in logic.

"Look!" he shouted, pointing at the blood with frantic urgency. "Stop crying! You look just like a cowboy that got shot!"

The psychological shift was instantaneous and total. The tears stopped mid-stream. I puffed out my chest, wiped my eyes with my good arm, and thought, *wow, I really do look like a cowboy.* The wound was no longer an injury; it was a badge of honor, a piece of the narrative. I marched into the house with all the swagger of a wounded gunslinger and proudly announced, "Mom, look! I look like a cowboy bleeding!"

The last thing I heard as Mom's face shifted from confusion to motherly alarm was the sound of Joe's own terrified crying as he received his "cowboy" punishment. Meanwhile, I was not looking for a bandage; I was searching for my dime-store cowboy hat to complete the look.

That day, Joe's quick thinking was the medicine that kept my spirit from breaking, even if my skin did not fare as well. It was an early lesson in the power of perspective: the same event can be a tragedy or a triumph, depending entirely on the story you choose to tell yourself about the "blood on your sleeve."

The Three Amigos

For me, Billy, and Joe, Halloween was always a season of excitement. Regardless of how lean the year had been, we always managed to pull together a costume for the school carnival and the ultimate *coup de grace*—the night of trick-or-treating.

I can clearly remember those store-bought plastic costumes that came in thin cardboard boxes. The moment you opened them, you were hit with that overwhelming, chemical scent of vinyl and Plastic. The masks were the true test of endurance; they were flimsy things, held together by nothing more than two silver staples and a thin, white rubber band that had a lifespan of about ten minutes before it inevitably snapped under the pressure of a child's anticipation.

The struggle with those masks was real. After a few minutes of walking in the neighborhood, the condensation from your own breath would build up inside the plastic shell, making the interior slick and wet against your skin. We always gave up on the "secret identity" and pulled the masks off, letting them hang around our necks like plastic bibs.

The candy we gathered was more than just sugar; to us, it was like a fine treasure we had unearthed from the depths of the neighborhood. We used old pillowcases as our sacks, and by the end of the night, the weight of the haul would make our arms ache in the best possible way.

When we finally made it back home, the air thick with the smell of autumn and the adrenaline of the hunt, we would dump the entire bounty onto the living room floor. It was a literal mountain of sugar, a kaleidoscopic pile of wrappers that shimmered under the house lights. We would sit there for a moment, simply marveling at our loot —a physical representation of miles walked, and doorbells rung.

Then, the feast began. We would gorge ourselves on the spoils of the night, diving into Snickers bars, M&M's, and the occasional Blow Pop. I remember the sharp, electric sizzle of Pop Rocks as they crackled and danced on our tongues, a sensation that felt like tiny fireworks in our mouths.

Yet, even amid our sugar-induced euphoria, we stayed surprisingly vigilant. We were the generation raised on urban legends, so we carefully inspected every single piece of candy. We were looking for those legendary razor blades we had been warned mean-spirited people were hiding inside the chocolate or the fruit. It was a classic piece of neighborhood lore—the "Stranger Danger" of the holiday—that never quite dampened our spirits, but it certainly kept us on high alert as we feasted.

Looking back, we never celebrated Halloween for the monsters, the ghouls, or the terror; we were not interested in the holiday's darkness. For us, the celebration was entirely about the haul. We celebrated the candy.

Day Camp

For a few summers, we were lucky enough to attend the YMCA day camp together. The setting was the thick, mysterious forest of Ambrosia Springs on the grounds of Fort Sill. It was there, under the canopy of Oklahoma timber, that we received our first formal training in the skills of the outdoors: archery, BB gun marksmanship, and the art of navigating wilderness.

One of our camp counselors was a master of the campfire tale, spinning wild, fascinating stories that felt terrifyingly real in the flickering light. He told us of the Witches' Well (the Ambrosia Springs well house, which was used to hang a witch when Fort Sill was a cavalry outpost) and the gruesome legend of Joseph E. Bull. The story went that Bull was an Army helicopter pilot who crashed deep in the woods. To escape the wreckage, he had to pull his own arm free, losing his mind in the agony of the ordeal. The story claimed he sharpened the protruding bone of his limb into a primitive hunting tool, prowling the forest as a feral ghost. According to the counselor, if you listened closely to the wind in the trees, you could hear the only word the pilot could still remember, screamed into the void: "BULL!"

I lost many nights of sleep to those stories, yet I remember day camp with a special fondness. We spent our days swimming in cold creeks, roasting marshmallows over crackling campfires, and creating art from the sticks and ropes we found in the brush.

The Night Walk

The final night of camp was the pinnacle of the summer. We would gather for an evening ceremony around a massive bonfire, where our parents were invited to watch us receive certificates for completing our "good camper" tasks. Once the parents left, the real test began. We would settle into our sleeping bags for an overnight stay, but not before the "night walk."

I will never forget trekking through the pitch-black woods with nothing but a small, dim flashlight. Suddenly, out of the dense weeds, "Joseph E. Bull" himself leaped into our path, screaming "BULL!" at the top of his lungs. I am not sure what travels faster than the speed of light, but that night, I am certain I broke the record. I sprinted through the woods, straight back to my sleeping bag, where I burrowed deep and spent at least an hour praying for dawn. It was, without a doubt, one of the most fun and terrifying moments of my entire youth.

However, the summer was not without its scars. Because we were divided by age, we each built our own camps in secluded areas of the forest. Joe, being the oldest, was with the more senior group. Unlike the kids with fancy plastic lunchboxes, Billy, Joe, and I always carried our food in simple brown paper bags.

One of the boys in Joe's camp thought it would be funny to snatch Joe's lunch sack and toss it into the flames. Once the bag was engulfed in fire, the boy pulled it out with a stick. A sudden gust of wind caught the flaming paper and blew it directly onto Joe's head.

The result was horrific: Joe suffered second-degree burns across his head, face, and neck. Being in my own camp, I did not find out until we boarded the bus for the ride home. The counselors told us Joe had been burned and rushed to the hospital. My young imagination ran wild; I spent the entire bus ride home terrified, picturing Joe with a face burned charcoal black and all his hair gone. I prayed desperately until the moment I walked through our front door.

To my immense relief, Joe was sitting there eating a popsicle, his face and neck coated in soothing lotion. He was okay.

The three of us—Joe, Billy, and I—remained inseparable, a three-man unit through countless adventures. That bond lasted until the inevitable happened: Joe discovered girls. Suddenly, the woods and the creeks were replaced by a preoccupation with his appearance. He started using Aqua Net hairspray to keep his feathered hair perfectly parted and immobile, even in the face of an Oklahoma gale-force wind. Our trio had changed, but the foundation of those years at Ambrosia Springs remained.

Lessons Galore

We grew up tough, forged in the heat and dust of a neighborhood that demanded resilience. It was a place where the lines of our lives were drawn by necessity rather than heritage; we played alongside kids who were just as poor as we were, coming from every imaginable background. In our world, there was no racial divide—there was only the shared reality of the struggle. Poverty was the great equalizer, a common language we all spoke fluently. We did not see a friend's skin color as much as we saw the holes in their shoes or the dirt under their fingernails, because we were all looking in the same mirror.

It was not the best neighborhood by any stretch of the imagination. The houses were weathered, the pavement was cracked, and the air often felt heavy with the unspoken pressures of our parents' lives. To survive that environment, we played hard. We threw ourselves into the street with a frantic, relentless intensity, using sports as a necessary outlet to burn off our excess energy and a mounting, unspoken angst that we did not yet have the words to describe.

A game of touch football or a makeshift basketball hoop became our retreat—a place where the frustrations of a lean kitchen or a quiet house could be channeled into a sprint or a tackle. We were not just playing for the sake of the game; we were outrunning our circumstances, one play at a time.

We were situated on the south side of town, nestled deep within the lowest economic bracket and the highest crime rate. The air there felt different—heavy with the scent of asphalt, cheap exhaust, and the underlying tension of a place where everyone was just trying to get by. Occasionally, the night air would be shattered by the sound of loud fights and domestic arguments echoing from the houses nearby. Even the occasional gunshot was a sound we learned to recognize early on—a sharp, dry crack that meant it was time to move away from the windows. I remember being warned specifically to watch out for a teenager named Rufus, who prowled our neighborhood. The legend of Rufus was dark and terrifying: word on the street was that he had once set someone on fire just for crossing his path. I am not sure how much of that was neighborhood myth and how much was cold fact, but my friends and I were always on high alert, scanning the sidewalks for any sign of him.

The Eye on the Corner

Living on a corner lot provided us with a bit of breathing room, leaving us with only one immediate neighbor directly beside us, an elderly couple who, by all objective accounts, were incredibly kind to our family throughout the years. The husband was an imposing, big-bodied man with a crown of shock-white hair and a voice that carried a surprisingly gentle, melodic tone. His wife, however, was his physical opposite: shorter and more heavily set.

While the husband was defined by his kindness, my memories of the wife were dominated by a single, unsettling feature—she had a pronounced lazy eye. No matter where my mother stood while chatting with her over the fence or on the porch, that wandering eye never seemed to follow the conversation. Instead, it stayed fixed in my direction, tracking my every move with a mind of its own.

As a child, I tried to convince myself I was just overthinking things, but the mystery took a darker turn thanks to my brother Joe. With the classic, ruthless wit of an older sibling, he leaned into my discomfort, whispering that she did not just watch me during the day—he claimed she watched me even when I was asleep. That was all the confirmation my young mind needed. From that moment on, the "kind neighbor" became a figure of silent, ocular surveillance. I kept a very respectful, wide distance from her and that unblinking gaze, a self-imposed exile that lasted until the day I finally moved away.

The Lot

Directly across the street sat an empty, overgrown field that served as our makeshift sports arena and a sprawling wildlife adventure area. Though it was no more than half a city block in size, to my young eyes, it was a vast, untamed frontier—my own personal Australian Outback. The tall, yellowed grass was our brush, and the dirt patches were our stadiums.

That field was the neighborhood kids' central gathering place. We would converge there to play football and baseball, making do with whatever battered equipment we could scavenge, borrow, or share. Often, I found myself trailing after Billy and his friends. They were two years older and significantly bigger than me, but their size did not intimidate me; if anything, it made me crave their acceptance even more. I wanted to prove that I belonged in their world, regardless of my age or stature.

I will never forget one afternoon joining Billy and his rag-tag group for a game of football. They did not go easy on me just because I was younger; in that neighborhood, "easy" did not exist. They tackled me with a force that knocked the wind out of my lungs, pinning me into the hard-packed Oklahoma earth. In the heat of the collision, a sharp, searing pain shot through my arm like a lightning bolt.

I found out later it was broken—the first of what would become a long, storied collection of plaster casts. Even as the pain set in and the swelling began, I would not have traded that moment for anything. I wanted to be where the action was, regardless of the physical cost. It was a badge of honor, a sign that I had stepped into the ring and survived.

Looking back now through the lens of a parent, I find myself wondering how many times my mother simply shook her head in disbelief while doing her level best to keep us from total self-destruction. I know now that she must have been in a state of constant prayer for our safety, acting as the silent, spiritual constant in our turbulent lives. We were a whirlwind of motion, rarely still and always plotting the next stunt, usually with Joe acting as the primary ringleader. He had a knack for finding the razor's edge of trouble, but in fairness, I cannot pin it all on him. I had my own streak of mischief and a healthy share of self-initiated trouble that kept the local doctors busy and my mother on her knees in prayer.

The Thirsty Earth

One day, while sober, my dad was in the backyard mowing the "lawn"—which, in our yard, was mostly a collection of stubborn weeds and prickly crabgrass. He finished his work and left to run a quick errand, leaving the equipment unattended. The lawnmower sat there in the sweltering heat, ticking as it cooled down, parked right next to a bright red can of gasoline and a white plastic funnel.

To a bored young boy with an overactive imagination, those were not just tools for maintenance; they were an invitation to an experiment.

I took the funnel and shoved it deep into red dirt just behind the back door of the house, where it was shaded and kept the ground soft. I unscrewed the cap of the gas can, the heavy fumes rising in the heat, and poured a little gasoline into the funnel. I watched with wide eyes as it disappeared instantly into the earth. I remember thinking how fast it vanished. It was like the ground was parched, thirsty for something other than rain.

I wondered: if I put more, would it disappear as fast? So, I poured more... same result. I poured more, fascinated by how the red dirt swallowed the fuel, soaking into the subterranean layers of our yard. Eventually, I got bored with the liquid itself and decided to see what would happen if I introduced a little excitement to the equation.

I ran into the kitchen, my heart hammering against my ribs with the thrill of the forbidden. I managed to grab a box of wooden matches without Mom seeing, my small fingers fumbling with the cardboard. I ran back outside, pulled the funnel out of the ground, and stood over the dark, damp hole I had created. I struck the match on the side of the box, watched the sulfur flare into a tiny orange flame, and dropped it straight into the hole where the funnel had been.

POOF!

The world turned orange. The gasoline had not just gone down; it had spread out through the porous soil like a subterranean lake. The whole yard around me erupted in a five-foot diameter of flame. I panicked, the heat singeing the hair on my arms. I ran to the back door and stuck my head in, yelling the first lie that came to mind: "MOM, SOMEONE STARTED A FIRE!"

She ran out, saw the ring of fire, and reacted with the practiced speed of a woman used to disasters. She grabbed an old rug and beat the flames into submission. Once the fire was out, she looked at me with a look that saw right through my "someone" story. "Someone, huh? Wait till your dad gets home."

I did what I always did: I ran into the house and crawled under the kitchen table. I waited for what seemed like hours, imagining every torture and punishment I had seen in old war movies. I was terrified.

When the front door finally creaked open, I jumped. I watched from my wooden sanctuary as my dad's heavy work boots walked into the kitchen. My mom's shoes met him.

"Your son started a fire in the back yard with the gas you left next to the mower," she said.

This was it. The end. I debated whether to plead for mercy or commit hara-kiri. I waited for the table to be flipped over and for the hand of justice to find me. I was shocked when I heard his quiet, tired voice.

"Did it burn anything?"

When my mom told him it had not, his response left me more shaken than a belt would have. He said, "Well, Hell Fire, out of all of them, I did not think he would do that."

The disappointment in his voice was a physical weight. I had plenty of spankings in my time—and I deserved every single one—but that moment of disappointment left the biggest impression on me, more than any belt ever could.

Barefoot

Growing up, I spent my days entirely barefoot, my soles becoming leathered and toughened by the constant contact with the dirt and gravel of our neighborhood. Most of our group spent their time barefoot; we were well-accustomed to the rocks and the searing heat of the asphalt beneath our feet. Wherever we went, we went without shoes, whether indoors or out.

Mac's grocery store was situated about half a mile away, and we would often make the trek there without a second thought about shoes. The transition was always startling: the icy, smooth floor inside the store provided a sharp, blissful contrast to the punishing heat of the asphalt and concrete we had just navigated. Under the unrelenting Oklahoma sun, the black tar used to fill street cracks would often bubble and liquefy, forcing us to watch our steps carefully to avoid the sticky, stinging mess. While being barefoot had its benefits, it also had its drawbacks.

The Forbidden Canal

Beyond the back porch lay a yard that held its own stories. There was an old, weathered one-bedroom 'house' on the property where Jackie and Mike lived for a time as they transitioned into adulthood. When it was not occupied by family, Mom and Dad would rent it to soldiers from the nearby base to scrape together a little extra rent.

At the far edge of the yard, the earth dipped into a shallow city canal. Most of the time, it was a dry, rocky scar in the land, but when the heavy rains came, it transformed into a rushing vein of muddy water. It only stayed in that form for a few years during my early childhood, but it stayed long enough to leave its mark on me—literally.

Despite our freedom to roam, there was one boundary that was non-negotiable. Mom had been incredibly explicit with her warning: **"Do NOT go into that canal."** She was not just being overprotective; she knew the reality of my situation. She knew I would be barefoot and understood exactly what that murky runoff carried. Beneath the deceptively soft silt lay a graveyard of hazards: shards of broken glass, torn and rusted metal, and sharp, barbed stones just waiting to slice through a young boy's foot. In her mind, that canal was not a playground; it was a trap.

I heeded her words for exactly as long as it took to watch Joe, Billy, Darlene, and Mary scramble down the bank. They were hunting for treasures: crawdads with waving pinchers, translucent tadpoles, and whatever "gold" the city runoff had deposited. The temptation was too much. I rambled down the side, my bare toes gripping the slick mud, and stepped into the sitting pools of water.

I had just spotted a cluster of tadpoles, their little tails flickering in the murk, when a searing, electric heat shot through the bottom of my foot. I looked down, and the water around my heel began to bloom a brilliant, terrifying red. A deep gash ran from my heel to the ball of my foot, sliced open by a hidden shard of glass.

I let out a scream that reached the next block. My siblings swarmed me instantly, their play forgotten. They hauled me to the edge of the bank, blood pouring out of the wound and staining the rocks. Someone, either Billy or Joe, sprinted to get our old red wagon. They hoisted me into the metal bed, and the "ambulance" ride began.

They ran toward the house, pushing and pulling the wagon with everything they had, their voices rising in a chorus of "Wee-ooo, wee-ooo!" mimicking the sirens of a real emergency. The memory is a blur of vibrating metal, the singsong wailing of my brothers and sisters, and the sight of my own blood pooling at the bottom of the wagon.

The next thing I remember is the interior of our old car. Mom was driving with a focused, terrifying intensity toward the hospital down the street. Darlene was in the seat with me, her face pale, pressing a white towel firmly against my foot. The towel did not stay white for long.

In the ER, the world became a series of bright lights and cold surfaces. I remember being strapped down—a small boy against the strength of a doctor and several nurses—as they prepared to stitch the skin back together. The sting of the needle and the tug of the thread felt infinitely worse than the first cut. To escape the pain, I stared at a black and yellow flashlight sitting on a nearby desk. I focused on its colors, its shape, its stillness. I think, in a way, I was already teaching myself how to "go somewhere else"—how to leave my body behind when the world became too painful to inhabit.

6

THE FIRM FOUNDATION OF MOM

The drafts in our house were not just uncomfortable; they were a threat to my health. My lungs, weakened by the dampness and the constant shifts in temperature, seemed to be a magnet for infection. I suffered through bout after bout of pneumonia, my chest rattling with every breath.

When I was about five, Mom took me to a free clinic. I was a mess— my throat was raw, and the lymph nodes in my neck had swollen until they felt like hard marbles under my skin. The doctor was a man who looked like he had not slept in a decade, a man worn down by the endless procession of impoverished, sick children. He looked at me not as a child, but as a problem to be solved with clinical detachment.

He turned to my mother and spoke with a cold finality that sucked the air out of the room. "He is constantly sick," he said. "He is never going to live to be twelve years old unless you take those tonsils out."

The silence that followed was heavy. To that doctor, it was a standard medical opinion, a routine recommendation for a chronic case. But he did not know our history. He did not know that my mother had already stood by a hospital bed and watched her firstborn son, Ronnie, bleed to death after that very same "routine" surgery.

I felt the room begin to vibrate. I looked at my mother, and I swear I saw actual flames behind her eyes. Every ounce of repressed grief for Ronnie, every fear she had ever harbored for my survival, and every bit of her fierce Pentecostal faith rose up at once. She did not just get angry; she became a force of nature.

She stood up, her shadow looming over the seated doctor, and looked him square in the eye. Her voice did not shake with tears; it thundered with the authority of a woman who had decided she would not lose another child to a blade.

"That is a LIE!" she bellowed. "He will LIVE and NOT die, and he will outlive you!"

She grabbed my arm with a grip like iron—a grip that told me she was never letting go—and marched me out of that clinic. We never went back. The medical world had failed her once, and she decided right then to trust the Great Physician instead. From that day on, she would pray for me through every fever, every rattle in my chest, and every sleepless, wheezing night. She had declared my life a victory, and in that drafty, broken house, her faith became the only insulation we had left.

The Texas Oasis

Every summer, from the time I was eight until after I graduated high school, I lived in Texas with my sister Darlene and my brother-in-law, Phil. To my brothers and me, they were a literal saving grace. They lived in apartments in Wichita Falls and Arlington, Texas. To us, coming from a house where the wind blew through the walls, they were palaces.

It was with them that we experienced central heat and air for the first time. I remember standing over the vent, feeling the cool, consistent hum of the AC, and thinking we had moved into the future. No swamp coolers that just moved the humidity around; no gas heaters that left you shivering three feet away. We loved it! We ate at fast-food restaurants—luxuries that were once-a-year treats back home—and, for the first time, felt like humans instead of just the "poor kids" from the drafty house.

As mentioned earlier, Phil was truly one of a kind. Next to my mother, he had the biggest heart and the best laugh I had ever heard. I know now that God sent them not just to take care of us, but to give my mom some much-needed time to herself and support. She had been carrying the weight of eight children and a husband lost in a bottle; Darlene and Phil provided the relief valve that kept her from breaking.

While I mention Darlene and Phil specifically because of those Texas summers, I know they were not the only ones. My other older brothers and sisters stepped in many times to provide for us. As the youngest, I was not always privy to the specific incidents or the heavy sacrifices they made in their own young adult lives to ensure the "littles" had what they needed, but I felt the warmth of their support like a constant sun. Our family was a net; when one part of it was frayed, the others pulled together to make sure no one fell through. There are so many memories that come flooding back during that time... some have changed a bit over the years, the edges softened, but the same emotions can be evoked with a single thought.

Miracles in Newspaper Wrapping

We did not have much, but we had each other. It was not always pretty, and it certainly was not "nice" in the way the world defines it, but God took loving care of us. The provisions in our lives often arrived in the form of a knock on the door, which we siblings saw as pure, unadulterated miracles.

The clothes we wore and almost every gift we received were from Goodwill. The toys were usually missing a piece or had a cracked limb, but we did not mind because we did not know any better. To us, a toy with a missing wheel was just a toy that had seen some "combat." A lot of times, our presents were wrapped with newspapers or magazine pages. I remember the smell of newsprint on Christmas morning, the black ink rubbing off on our fingers as we tore into our treasures.

Thanksgivings were a special time because we were out of school and could wake up to the sights, sounds, and smells of a kitchen in high gear. One Thanksgiving in particular stands as the ultimate definition of the grace that followed us. I remember waking up and walking into the kitchen to see my mother sitting at the table. She had a pained, hollow look on her face—the look of a mother who wanted to give her children a feast but was staring at empty cupboards and an empty refrigerator. The silence in the kitchen was deafening.

Suddenly, there was a knock. My brother Joe, who was about twelve at the time, went to answer it. He came back into the kitchen carrying an aluminum baking tray with a thawed turkey and a bag full of groceries. He said someone had just left it on the porch and disappeared into the morning mist. We were on cloud nine! We were so excited for our Thanksgiving meal that had appeared out of thin air.

It was not until years later that the mystery was solved. Darlene and Phil had driven an hour from Wichita Falls, Texas, in the pre-dawn darkness just to place that feast on our porch and slip away before they could be thanked. They did not want the credit; they wanted us to have the joy.

The Windowpane Stockings

I remember another Christmas that started with a hollow space beneath the tree. There were no brightly wrapped boxes or ribbons to be found. Mom sat us down, her voice steady and warm, as she explained that we would not be having "traditional" presents that year. Instead, she told us we were going to do something "different and fun."

Following her lead, we took our regular, everyday socks—the ones we wore to school and play—and nailed them over the windowsill to serve as our makeshift stockings. She filled them with assortments of nuts and simple penny candy. We were not disappointed; we were genuinely thrilled. In the world we inhabited, a handful of nuts and a few pieces of Christmas candy felt like a massive win. We were content with what we had.

The Christmas Miracle

But as the evening settled in, there was a sudden, unexpected knock at the door. When it swung open, a man dressed in a full, slightly weathered Santa Claus costume stepped inside. He carried a heavy, bulging bag that seemed to groan under its own weight. He did not say much—his presence was more about action than words. With quiet, purposeful kindness, he reached into his bag and handed out individual presents to each of us.

Just as quickly as he had arrived, he vanished back into the dark Lawton night, the frigid air swirling behind him as the door closed.

To this day, none of my siblings—nor my parents before they passed away—ever discovered the identity of that mysterious visitor. I am certain it was God doing what He does best: stepping into our lack and blessing us in ways we could not even conceive. It was a reminder that even when we thought we were forgotten, we were being watched over.

Terrible Tuesday

Then came that Tuesday in April 1979. I was ten years old. The day started deceptively normal. When we came home from school, it was sunny, though a few clouds hung low on the horizon. My dad was in his usual spot on the porch, smoking a cigarette and watching the horizon. He had an internal barometer that most Oklahomans develop—a sense of when the air feels "tight."

He told us to check the storm cellar for any standing water. Our cellar was a relic—an old concrete hole in the ground with cracks in the walls that invited the water every time it rained. It was always moist and cold down there, the perfect habitat for brown recluse spiders and giant, slimy slugs. I remember thinking it was too sunny for storms, but Billy and I—the only kids left at home at the time, since Joe had gone to stay with Jackie and Debbie in Alaska—did as we were told. We checked the water level, spent some time pouring salt on the slugs just to watch them dissolve, and reported back that it was okay. An hour later, the world changed.

The Green Sky

The sky did not just turn dark; it shifted into a sickly, bruised green— the unsettling color of a deep copper patina. Then, as if a giant hand had reached up and turned a dial, the sun was extinguished entirely. It was replaced by a pitch-black darkness that felt heavy and oppressive against your skin. The wind, which usually howled and whistled through the eaves, suddenly stopped. Everything went dead quiet. No birds chirped, no dogs barked... There was only a terrifying, pressurized silence that seemed to vibrate in your ears.

Our storm shelter was inside a small wooden shed built from two sides of the house, so only 2 walls and a roof were needed to enclose it. My dad kept all his painting equipment and anything that needed to be out of the rain in here. This included his old green Coleman lantern that he grabbed after opening the cellar door. His voice was steady—calm but urgent. "Get in the cellar," he commanded.

We scrambled down into the damp, earthy darkness of the cellar and pulled the heavy wooden door shut above us, slamming it with a finality that signaled our isolation from the world above. I can still vividly recall the sharp, chemical smell of the lantern fuel, the hiss as he pumped up the pressure, and the wicks catching fire, casting a flickering, amber glow against the encroaching darkness.

The Storm Above

At once, the silence was shattered as we heard the wind begin to howl and the storm sirens start to scream. The storm cellar was equipped with a tiny 10" x 4" ventilation window at ground level, covered only by a thin mesh screen. Through that small, narrow slit, we listened as the roar intensified into something primal.

Then the rain started—not in individual drops, but as a violent deluge that pounded the parched earth with relentless force. It was quickly followed by the impact of hail outside and against the cellar window, each strike sounding like a hammer blow from above.

Tucked away in the belly of the Oklahoma red dirt, we waited in the damp darkness. We huddled together, listening to the world above as the weather unleashed a violent, unbridled fury. It felt personal—as if the sky itself were possessed by a dark, roiling rage, lashing out as though it were truly mad at the earth.

Then we heard it. It was not the sound of the wind anymore. It was the sound of a freight train running full speed toward our house. The pressure inside the cellar dropped so low our ears popped painfully; it felt like the air was being sucked right out of our lungs. We watched through the tiny window as debris began to fly—sticks, rocks, and shards of glass slammed against the screen, blowing dust and muddy water onto us. Suddenly, a large board flew against the window and wedged itself perfectly over the opening, sealing us in and safe from any debris.

The "train" grew so loud that the ground vibrated. We covered our ears and prayed, my mother's voice steady in the dark, calling out for protection. And then, as quickly as it had arrived, the roar faded into the distance. Silence returned.

The Aftermath

The transition from the safety of the storm cellar to the reality of the surface was a shock that redefined my understanding of permanence. When we finally managed to heave the heavy cellar door open, the world I had known just moments before was gone. The sun was beginning to peek through the retreating, bruised clouds, casting a cruel, sparkling light on the wreckage—a brightness that felt like an insult to the devastation below it.

Our house had not just been damaged; it had been effectively erased from the landscape. The modest, cramped rooms where we had eaten our meals, shared our dreams, and sought refuge from the world were reduced to a cluttered, skeletal footprint of splintered wood and twisted linoleum.

As I picked through the debris, I saw the fragments of our daily life scattered like confetti. Our bunk bed, the very site of countless hours spent whispering stories of adventure and faraway travel with Joe and Billy, lay overturned and broken, its wooden frame snapped like kindling. The heavy metal barracks fan that had roared us to sleep, shielding us from the Oklahoma heat, was bent in half, its blades silent and useless.

Even the sturdy table I had taken refuge under so many times during our "cowboy" games or dad's drinking binges was smashed into unrecognizable pieces. The mismatched collection of cups, plates, and utensils we had carefully gathered over the years—each one representing a small victory of survival—was simply gone, swallowed by the wind.

A Neighborhood Transformed

Our home at 415 Monroe was simply gone. Standing where our front door used to be, the entire neighborhood was completely unrecognizable; it looked like a literal war zone, a landscape stripped of its familiarity and replaced with the gray wreckage of our lives. The storm's violence had rewritten the street's geography in a matter of seconds.

What was most haunting, however, was the sheer, boggling nature of the twister's path. The destruction followed no logical pattern, operating instead with a cruel, erratic, selective power. Our house was leveled, reduced to a splintered, debris-filled footprint. Yet, in a twist of fate that was impossible to reconcile, the neighbor's house directly next to us stood completely untouched—as if the storm had simply stepped over it. Then, just as abruptly as it had spared one home, the tornado slammed back down, leaving the house next to theirs destroyed.

It was a mosaic of ruin and survival. Seeing a neighbor's curtains still fluttering in a window while our own walls had been carried off into the Oklahoma sky was a sight that defied explanation. It left us standing in the middle of a broken street, staring at the lottery of the wind, and wondering how a force so massive could be so impossibly precise in its devastation.

Power lines lay snaked across the ground like downed serpents, and water—whether from broken mains or the lingering torrential rain—covered everything up to our ankles. The trees that once defined our property and provided us with shade were now stripped bare of their leaves and even their bark, lying on their sides like fallen, defeated giants. The neighbor's house diagonally across the four-way intersection from us was turned 180 degrees. The back door now faced forward, and the front door faced back. The surreal nature of the destruction was everywhere. In the branches of the fallen trees, clothes were tangled like tattered flags of a lost cause. Our car was punctured with boards and branches, while every window had been shattered into a thousand tiny diamonds of safety glass that covered the seats.

Most shocking of all was the horse trailer parked in our backyard for my dad to paint. It was simply gone—erased from its footprint. We found it much later, two blocks away from its original spot, beaten and dented by various missiles from the storm. The force needed to move and manipulate steel in that way was a terrifying reminder of our own fragility.

As I stood amidst the wreckage, I felt the weight of the devastation. It was a scene of total loss, a physical manifestation of the storms we had faced internally as a family. Yet, even in the middle of a literal disaster zone, there was a sense of survival. The storm had passed, and though it had taken the trailer and stripped the trees, it had not taken us. We were left with the red dirt of Lawton beneath the debris, ready to begin the long, slow process of rebuilding what the wind had tried to erase.

The Living Sermon

The atmosphere was heavy and suffocating, thick with the overwhelming smell of wet earth and the sharp, terrifying scent of escaping natural gas. The silence of the aftermath was broken by my mother's frantic voice; she was yelling for my dad to turn the gas off at once. Our stove had been torn violently away from the wall and carried off, leaving the pipes exposed and hissing a steady stream of gas into the open air. In that moment, standing in the mud and the ruins of my childhood, I realized for the first time that the world could be broken in an instant, and that the only thing left standing was the family beside me.

I have many images from that day, but the one that is burned into my soul is my mother in the aftermath. She did not sit on a stump and mourn the loss of her few possessions. She did not cry over the walls or the roof. She was immediately out in the mud, her hands stained dark by the red Oklahoma earth, searching through piles of ruined Goodwill clothes and debris. She was not looking for her own things; she was looking for us, and then for the neighbors.

In those moments, watching her move through the wreckage with such selfless determination, the scriptures stopped being words on a page and became a living reality. People talk about the love of Jesus, but that day, I saw it in the flesh. It was not in a cathedral or a sermon; it was in my mother's tired back and her muddied hands as she pulled our lives back together. Her love was the living, breathing proof of the Gospel—a shepherd looking for what was lost in the storm. We had lost every stick of furniture we owned. We were dirt-poor and now, technically, homeless. But as I stood in the debris, I realized we were not abandoned. The cellar had kept our bodies safe, and my mother's love kept our spirits whole. I learned that when you lose everything, the only thing that truly survives is the spirit of those who refuse to let you fall.

That day changed the trajectory of my life. It was a lesson in service and sacrifice. My mother was the woman who told a doctor I would live, and then she spent her life proving it through the wreckage of poverty and storms. Standing in that debris, I made a silent vow. I decided I would follow the nudging I had always felt; I would be a protector. I would be the one who stood watch so that others would not have to stand alone in the ruins. I would eventually put on a uniform, but the heart of the man in that uniform was forged in the green sky and the red mud of Lawton.

Loss

The day the tornado struck Lawton, the world turned upside down. My brother Mike lived all the way across town, but as soon as the storm passed, he made his way to us. I can still remember the sight of him running toward our home through the scattered debris; his face was as white as a sheet, as though he expected to find the absolute worst. Without hesitation, he jumped in to help us salvage whatever belongings we could gather from the wreckage. Since our home was no longer an option, we stayed with him until we finally found a new place to live.

While we were dealing with the aftermath in Lawton, Wichita Falls, Texas—just an hour away—was enduring the worst tornado in its history on that very same day. My sister Mary and her husband David were driving home from Arlington, Texas, right through Wichita Falls, when they saw the historic destruction. They managed to navigate the chaos of the ravaged streets and reach Lawton. I will never forget the relief of seeing them running down our street just to check on us. After everything that had happened that day, I was so incredibly happy to see with my own eyes that they were okay.

We were safe, but others were not so lucky. I found out later that eight of my classmates had lost their homes that day. Many were seriously injured, including broken backs, arms, and legs. Most devastatingly, three people lost their lives. One was particularly close to my heart. Our good friends, the Millers, lived on the corner of 4th and Jefferson. Their house was hit directly while they were all inside. Their 10-month-old niece, Stephanie, was killed.

Stephanie and I shared a birthday—February 9th. She was 10 months old, and I was 10 years old. Every time we went to the Millers to hang out with Butch, Mitzi, and Donnie, I would play with her. To see that family broken by the same wind that had spared us was a weight I did not know how to carry.

7

THE HORIZON OF THE WICHITA MOUNTAINS

If Chapter 6 was about the storm that cleared the landscape of my childhood, then Chapter 7 is about the long, slow climb out of the debris and my outward expansion past those majestic mountains. It is about the years of reconstruction—not just of walls and roofs, but of identity. Growing up in Lawton in the 1970s and 1980s meant living in a town that felt like a permanent extension of Fort Sill. The city's identity was wrapped in olive drab and the heavy, industrial smell of diesel.

The air was punctuated by the distant boom of artillery practice—a sound that, to a boy like me, felt more like a heartbeat than a warning. You did not just hear the boom; you felt it in your chest, a low-frequency vibration that rattled the windowpanes and reminded you that strength and protection were always nearby, even if they were loud and jarring. It was a constant reminder that we lived on the edge of a great power. Even then, I was learning about God and starting to understand that I was being conditioned to recognize the sound of a fortress.

Those mountains—the Wichitas—stood on the horizon like ancient, granite sentinels. They were monuments of rock and heat, an ominous boundary that marked the edge of the known world. These peaks were not just scenery; they were a silent witness to a history that felt both legendary and dangerous.

Over the decades, these mountains were well-known hunting grounds for the Plains tribes, including the Kiowa, Comanche, and Wichita Nations. For these Native American peoples, the range was more than just a landmark; it was a source of life and a spiritual stronghold. The peaks were frequented by iconic leaders such as the Apache Chief Geronimo—who spent his final years at nearby Fort Sill—and the legendary Comanche Chief Quanah Parker. Their legacies seem to linger in the very canyons and buffalo grass of the range, a reminder of a warrior spirit that refuses to be forgotten.

The Wichitas also served as a rugged hideaway for many "outlaws" who looked to disappear from the reach of the law. Figures like Jesse and Frank James, the infamous duo Bonnie and Clyde, and the Depression-era gangster Pretty Boy Floyd all used the badlands of Oklahoma as a hideout.

They were drawn to the labyrinth of boulders and hidden draws, running to the wild heart of the state to conceal themselves and their illicit gains. Growing up in the shadow of such history, you realized early on that these mountains were a place of refuge for both the righteous and the desperate. It was a land where the line between legend and reality was as thin as the mountain air, and where the echoes of the past—from the war cries of the Comanche to the muffled hoofbeats of an outlaw's horse—could still be felt if you knew how to listen.

They came to these peaks to disappear into the maze of rocks and boulders, stashing themselves and the treasure they had found periodically over the years. Growing up in their shadow, you could not help but feel that the mountains held secrets—that they were a place where a man could either find his destiny or lose himself entirely.

To a young boy, the Wichitas were a physical manifestation of the "Great Unknown." They stood for a frontier that needed respect and a sharp eye. They were not just rocks; they were the fortress of the desperate and the temple of the brave. As I looked at them, I realized that if I was going to cross those mountains and step into the world beyond, I would need more than just guts—I would need the skills of a scout and the protection of the One who laid the mountains' foundations.

To me, they stood for the mystery of what lay beyond Lawton, a world I was desperate to see but afraid to traverse without a map. They were beautiful, yes, but they were also intimidating, standing as the gatekeepers of the "great unknown."

I spent hours staring at those peaks, wondering if the life I was fashioned for was waiting on the other side of those granite walls. Little did I know that something in me was already being trained. I was learning to see the terrain, to respect the power of the artillery, and to understand that reconstruction is a process that requires patience and a solid foundation. The debris of the tornado had been cleared, but the landscape of my soul was just beginning to be shaped. I was a boy living in the shadow of a fortress, looking at a mountain, waiting for my orders to move out.

The Emergency Contact Faith

Looking back, I see with perfect clarity how God continued to bless us and provide for our every need, often using the hands of others to do the heavy lifting. Witnessing such consistent examples of kindness, love, mercy, and grace, one might assume I would have walked a flawless path with the Lord. But I did not.

I had given my life to Jesus at eight years old. I loved Him, I knew He existed, and I understood deeply that He wanted good for me, not harm. Yet time after time in church, different people would speak a "word" over me, all echoing the same haunting refrain: "You have the heart of a pastor; you are going to be a pastor; you are anointed to be a pastor."

In my young, stubborn mind, all I knew was that I **did not** want that life. I had no desire to scream and yell from a pulpit, and I certainly did not want Jimmy Swaggart's hair. Beyond the aesthetics, I was plagued by a sense of unworthiness. I knew the thoughts I had; I knew my own failings. I was convinced that God could not use someone as "bad" as me. Even then, I recognized how blessed I had been. I had seen the "green sky" and survived; I had seen the "turkey miracle" and been fed. But as I grew older and the turbulent hormones of adolescence kicked in, I found myself wanting to serve myself more.

Between Two Worlds

Throughout my teenage years, sports and girls consumed my entire focus. The discipline of my mother's faith began to feel like a tether I was desperate to cut. I started treating God like an emergency contact —a 911 operator I only dialed when I was in trouble, facing a failed test, or in desperate need of a favor. I was caught between two worlds: the deep-rooted faith my mother had planted in me like a sturdy oak, and the impulsive, shifting desires of a young man trying to be "somebody" in a town that felt far too small.

I became a "Sunday Christian" and a "Monday Me." I knew the sacred language of the pews, but during the week, I spoke only the language of the world. Despite my wandering, the truth I had seen as a child remained lodged in my soul. I knew God was real and wanted the best for me, but I was in a constant battle—struggling to get what I wanted while shoving God onto the back shelf.

. . .

The Requirement of Action

It is true that God blesses us, and He continues to do so faithfully. But I have learned the key: Mom, Phil, Darlene, and all those unknown "Santas" had to do more than just listen. They had to feel the Holy Spirit's nudge and do **something**. They had to get in the car. They had to buy the groceries. They had to put on the suit. They had to move beyond hearing and step into action.

God provides the manna, but someone still must go out into the field and gather it. He does His part with infinite grace, but we are called to do ours. Faith without feet stays stationary; they had to walk for the blessing to reach us.

The Recruiter's Door

They did their part, and I was blessed because of their obedience. And it was that realization—that faith requires legs, that protection requires a protector—that finally led me to the recruiter's door. I was tired of being the one who was looked after. I wanted to be the one doing the looking. I walked into the office looking for the path that put me out front, the path that required the most of me. I wanted to be a scout. In the military, the scout is the eyes and ears; they go where the danger is first to make the way safe for others.

I did not realize it at the time, but I had been scouting my whole life. I had been watching for the green sky to warn my family. I had been watching my mother's face to see if we were going to eat that night. I had been watching for the moments of grace in a hard world.

Finally, I reached the moment where I would stop treating God like a 911 operator and start treating Him like the Commander of my life. I realized that "Thy will be done" is not a request for God to do a magic trick; it is a commitment to be the instrument of that will.

I stepped onto that bus for Basic Training, leaving the Wichita Mountains in the rearview mirror. I went with the blood of Jesus as my shield and the realization that the years of being the "youngest in line" were over. It was finally time for me to stand at the front. It was finally time for me to do my part.

8

THE FORGE AND THE VALLEY

Fort Knox was the fire where my steel was tempered. If Lawton had been the raw material—the red clay and the stubborn resilience of a boy raised in a drafty house—then Kentucky was the furnace.

Leaving Oklahoma in 1987, I was eighteen years old, a lean kid with nothing but the clothes on my back, a small Bible, and the heavy, constant echo of my mother's prayers. Crossing the state line felt like crossing a physical barrier between my childhood and the man I was supposed to become. In Basic Training, the Army has a specific mission: they take everything that makes you different—your hair, your clothes, your sleep schedule, your very name—and they strip it away. They reduce you to a blank canvas of Army green. But for a kid who had grown up in a house where the walls barely held out the wind, where the foundation was shaky, and the future was uncertain, the rigid, uncompromising structure of the Army was strangely comforting. For the first time in my life, I knew exactly where my next meal was coming from, exactly where I was supposed to stand, and exactly what the rules were.

Being yelled at during basic training did not bother me in the slightest. By the time I stood before a drill sergeant, I had been seasoned by years of high-volume reprimands; I had been yelled at for as long as I could remember for one thing or another. My mother, however, was the exception. She never had to raise her voice to get a point across. She did not yell; she simply spoke with a specific, weighted tone, and I got the message loud and clear. Throughout my entire life, I did everything in my power to avoid disappointing her. The mere thought of her giving me a look of disappointment was enough to correct my behavior far more effectively than any physical discipline or spanking ever could.

My father was a different story entirely. He was a man who would yell quite a bit, drunk or sober, and I will never forget the morning I realized, halfway to school, that I had forgotten my math book. I stopped at Mac's grocery store and nervously used the store phone to call home, praying he might be willing to bring it to me. He absolutely let me have it over the phone, though he agreed to come. I waited there, heart racing, until he finally pulled up next to the store in his old work truck.

The moment I hopped into the truck's cab, the atmosphere was already electric with tension. He let loose at once, his voice booming in the cramped space as he shouted about how he did not have time to be "babysitting" me and how I needed to stop being so forgetful. I felt my spirit retreat; I simply zoned out, staring ahead as he continued his tirade. In the background, mocking the lecture's gravity, Don Williams blared **"Living on Tulsa Time"** from the radio.

Just as he was pulling out of the parking lot, the situation shifted from a verbal lashing to a physical disaster. A woman pulling into the lot overshot the entrance, her car plowing directly into the driver's side door of my dad's truck. The impact jolted the cab, but it was the silence afterward that was truly terrifying.

White-Hot Anger

He completely blew his top. He did not look at the other driver first; he turned on me, laying into me with everything he had.

"If you hadn't forgotten your blankety-blank book, this wouldn't have happened!" he screamed. His eyes were wide, and his voice hit that high pitch that it only reached when he was in the throes of white-hot, uncontrollable anger. "How are we supposed to pay to have this fixed?"

I felt horrible, a hollow pit forming in my stomach. I knew, logically, that I had not driven the other woman's car into us, but his fury made me feel responsible for the very movement of the stars. I sat there, paralyzed and staring silently out the window, while he scrambled out of the truck to confront the lady.

As the tension boiled over outside—the sound of raised voices and the heat of the Oklahoma afternoon—the lyrics continued to mock the moment from the speakers, indifferent to my misery: *"Gonna set my watch back to it, 'cause you know I been through it, living on Tulsa time."*

The Eyes and Ears

I arrived at Fort Knox to begin my journey toward becoming a **19 Delta—a Cavalry Scout.** In the complex hierarchy of the United States Army, scouts are truly a breed apart. We are the "Eyes and Ears" of the commander, operating in the high-stakes space between our own lines and the unknown.

Our mission is one of stealth and precision; we move ahead of the main armored force, often alone or in small, specialized teams. Our purpose is to find the enemy, map the treacherous terrain, and bring back the "ground truth" before the heavy divisions ever make contact. Even now, decades later, the lessons I learned in the Cavalry remain the pillars of my life. The discipline, the vigilance, and the tactical mindset continue to help me be a better leader, husband, father, and man.

The Trials of Basic Training

Basic Training was hot, and it played on me harder than any mental games the drill sergeants could devise. The heat was extreme, and we spent hours on vast concrete pads learning to march. Unfortunately, when someone messed up—which happened quite a bit—the entire group ended up doing push-ups on that scalding hot concrete until our arms gave out.

If the drill sergeants decided we were not performing to their standards, they would scream "GAS!" That was the signal to scramble for our protective masks. These were heavy black rubber masks with plastic windows and a hood designed to seal out nuclear, chemical, or biological elements. They featured two filters that you had to pull air through with every labored breath. Trying to breathe through those filters while performing "mountain climbers," push-ups, and various other punishments—all while sweating profusely inside the rubber and hood—was a different kind of hell I fought desperately to avoid.

Before I ever stepped foot on the bus for basic training, I had already received my first set of orders from my older brothers. Having survived the experience themselves, they taught me the golden rule of military survival: "blend in."

They warned me to never stick out or draw unnecessary attention to myself. The goal was to remain a faceless shadow in the crowd, ensuring the drill sergeants would spend their time and fury on the other recruits who were messing up. If I could stay invisible, I could avoid drawing their wrath down on me.

For a while, I was doing great. I was a ghost in the ranks—until the day the illusion of anonymity was shattered.

We were standing in formation, the air heavy with tension, when a drill sergeant's voice suddenly cut through the silence. "Guess what, privates! We have a celebrity in our midst!" he bellowed, his voice dripping with thick, menacing sarcasm. He barked again, "We have ELVIS PRESLEY with us!"

In that moment, my heart sank into my boots. They had discovered the secret I had carefully guarded my entire life: my middle name was Elvis.

My mother, in all her creative wisdom, had gifted me that name by combining her brother's name, Ellis, with her own nickname, LV. The math resulted in "Elvis." While that logic might have looked good on paper or in a baby book, it was a recipe for instant punishment in the world of basic training.

The drill sergeant wasted no time in extending a mock invitation. "Private Elvis, come up front! We all want to meet you!"

As I broke rank and ran to the front of the formation—facing 120 fellow soldiers and a gauntlet of 12 drill sergeants—I could feel the cold prickle of panic rising within me. The drill sergeant leaned in, ensuring the entire company could hear his next decree. "Private Elvis, I just want you to know... from this point on, you are our 'hunk a, hunk of burning love.' Now PUSH!"

Because of my middle name, he made the entire formation drop and do push-ups while I danced like Elvis Presley in front of everyone. I was no longer invisible; I was the reason 120 men were hitting the dirt.

From that point on, my cover was permanently blown. Whenever that drill sergeant caught sight of me, he would mockingly ask if I was "ready for a Blue Christmas" or if I was planning to go eat a peanut butter and "nana" sandwich. My brothers' advice had been sound, but no amount of blending in could hide me from the legacy of the King of Rock and Roll.

Every time the thick, soup-like Kentucky humidity threatened to choke me during training, I heard that doctor's voice from the free clinic ringing in my ears: "He'll never live to be twelve." As I pushed my body through the sucking mud and the gray dawn, I felt my mother's decree of "Life" pulsing in my chest like a second heartbeat. I was not just running for the Army; I was running against a death sentence that had been overturned by a mother's faith. With every step, I was proving that the doctor was a liar and that God was the truth.

The Physical Standard

To survive in the scout world, you must be in the best physical shape possible. The demands on a 19 Delta are relentless, requiring endurance, strength, and mental toughness. At the time, I viewed this requirement with quiet confidence. Given my background as a competitive athlete, I genuinely thought the physical rigors of the training would be a "piece of cake." I was young, I was fit, and I was ready—or so I thought.

While I served, Physical Training (PT) for a scout was far more than a morning exercise routine; it was a calculated form of torture. It was a refined system of stress and exertion designed with one primary goal: to weed out the weak and break those who did not possess the internal "wiring" to endure.

We lost about ten trainees in the first week alone. They simply could not keep up, or, more commonly, they could not learn to follow simple instructions while under the crushing weight of physical weakness and constant, high-volume yelling.

One trainee I will never forget was Private Hernandez from Paterson, New Jersey. He had a notable speech impediment and was constantly bragging about being a "New-Yor-rican." At the time, I had never heard the term, but he took immense pride in explaining that he was a Puerto Rican from New York. Even in the middle of basic training, I was already learning new things about the world outside of Lawton.

However, Hernandez struggled with the simplest tasks. He was perpetually in trouble with the Drill Sergeants, which, by the laws of the Army, meant the rest of us were in trouble, too. He would come out to formation—where the Drill Sergeants were just itching for one of us to have forgotten a detail—and he would inevitably have missed a spot shaving, left his boots untied, or forgotten his belt. Every single day, the entire platoon would get thrashed because of something Hernandez forgot or did not do correctly.

Finally, I decided to take his survival into my own hands. I resolved to make sure he was "squared away" for formation every morning as soon as I finished getting myself ready. I wanted to stop paying the price for his mistakes. One morning, I had him all set—uniform perfect, gear in place—ready to pass any inspection. I headed out to the formation, and Hernandez followed shortly after a quick trip to the latrine.

While standing at attention, your world is restricted; you can see only what is directly in front of you and hear only what is happening in the periphery. Suddenly, the silence was shattered. I heard a Drill Sergeant yelling at the top of his lungs, "Private Hernandez! Why are your glasses broken? Where is the arm of your glasses?"

To which Hernandez replied through his speech impediment, "Ith inthide, Dwill Thargent."

"GO GET IT FIXED NOW, PRIVATE HERNANDEZ! I DON'T CARE HOW, JUST DO IT!" the Drill Sergeant bellowed.

As soon as Hernandez scrambled inside, the rest of us were dropped into the push-up position. We stayed there, holding ourselves up, until he returned. My arms were burning, the lactic acid was screaming, and I just wanted to get on with the day's training.

Then it happened. I have never heard a human being yell as loudly or as violently as that Drill Sergeant did that day. The sound was so primal that I broke the position of attention to see what was happening. I watched as the Drill Sergeant snatched the glasses off Hernandez's face, threw them onto the concrete, and stomped them into a hundred pieces.

Then I saw the cause of the explosion. Hernandez had gone inside to "fix" the missing arm of his glasses just as he was ordered. He had accomplished this by using a massive diaper pin—complete with a bright, pink baby duck on the end—to hinge the arm back onto the frames.

In the high-stakes, hyper-masculine world of scout training, that little pink duck was the ultimate fuse. We were being forged into soldiers and warriors, yet there stood Hernandez, sporting a piece of nursery equipment on his face. It was the perfect example of the "broken wiring" the military was trying to find—and that day, the system found it.

Feet First

In those days, the Army's regulations on footwear were rigid and unforgiving, to say the least. The only time we were granted the luxury of athletic shoes was during the strictly designated hours of organized Physical Training (PT). Every other waking moment of our existence—whether we were double-timing it to the chow hall, rushing to the armory under a ticking clock, or traversing the rugged terrain between training sites—we had to run in heavy, black leather combat boots.

These were not the high-tech, ergonomic boots of the modern era. They were slabs of stiff leather with no cushioning, no arch support, and zero margin for error. Every strike of the heel against the pavement sent a shockwave through the shins and up the spine. For a soldier, your feet are your most vital piece of equipment, and mine were already compromised.

Since I am naturally flat-footed—a medical reality that, by the book, often disqualified potential recruits from service—I should not have been standing on that parade field at all. In many ways, I was an anomaly in the system.

My entry into the military was a result of a perfect, silent storm: a mix of my own determination to stay quiet during the pre-entry physical and the sheer luck of a harried doctor who never bothered to look down at my arches. I had managed to navigate the gauntlet of physical exams and slip through the intake process undetected. By the time the Army realized my feet were not built for the "standard" soldier's life, I had already been processed, sworn in, and shipped out to meet my destiny. I was in the fight now, whether my feet were ready for it or not.

But that success came with a heavy price tag, paid for in constant, throbbing pain. If you have never experienced the specific misery of shin splints, the best way I can describe it is this: it feels as though serrated knives are being driven deep into your shins with every single footfall.

Wearing combat boots was a brand-new experience for me, and pounding the unforgiving pavement of the training grounds in them made the agony unbearable. The leather was stiff, the soles were hard, and the impact vibrated through my bones.

The physical pain was a loud, screaming voice in my head. I wanted to quit every time my feet hit the ground. I wanted to stop every time the "knives" twisted in my shins. But as I ran, I realized there was something buried deep within my spirit—forged in the red dirt of Lawton or the wreckage of the tornado—that flatly refused to let me stop.

I was learning that a scout's greatest weapon is not his rifle or his vehicle; it is the bridge between his mind and his feet. I might have been flat-footed, but I was developing a soul that was "rough-terrain capable." I kept running, not because the pain stopped, but because my mission had already begun.

I am not, and will never be, a distance runner. My athletic identity was forged on the fields of my youth, defined by football, baseball, and basketball—sports characterized by explosive, anaerobic bursts of speed and quick pivots. I was built for the sprint, not the marathon. The Army, however, believed firmly in the "long haul."

From day one, the "explosive" world I knew was replaced by the grinding reality of five-mile runs. To the uninitiated, five miles might sound manageable, but it is a much greater distance than most realize—especially when you are covering that ground in heavy, unyielding combat boots on unforgiving asphalt. As our training progressed and our bodies began to harden, the miles stretched. Five became seven, and eventually, we were pushing through ten-mile slogs that had no end.

Agony, Misery, and Heartbreak

Just when I thought I had finally found a comfortable stride and a way to manage the pain in my shins, the drill sergeants introduced us to the "Three Sisters." Anyone who endured basic training at Fort Knox can attest to the deep-down hatred reserved for these three infamous hills. Their names were not hyperbole: Agony, Misery, and Heartbreak.

They were not merely geographical features on a Kentucky landscape; they were precision tools of psychological warfare. These were the steepest, most unforgiving inclines in the entire region, designed to sap the strength of the strongest legs. We would lean into the climb, our lungs burning like fire and our vision blurring from the exertion.

Just as we would finally struggle to the summit—gasping for oxygen and thinking the trial was over—the drill sergeants would often circle the formation back around. They would order us to run them all over again. It was in those moments that I realized the training was not just about physical fitness or cardiovascular health. It was about breaking the human will to discover exactly what lay underneath the surface. The Army did not just want a runner; they wanted a scout who could look at a mountain of Agony and keep his feet moving.

Cold November Rain

I did not think anything would be as hard as those hills, but I was very wrong. The true test came during our "field week," the culminating exercise in which we apply all the combat skills we have learned—map reading, calling for fire, camouflage, vehicle identification, weapon systems, stealthy movement—in a combat situation in the woods.

Our designated training location was more than 20 miles away, a distance we were expected to cover on foot with rucksacks weighing 50 pounds. However, fate (and the weather) had other plans. Forest fires had broken out in the primary training area, so our mission was diverted. We ended up road marching around our barracks and then heading into a dense, wooded plot just across the street called Strike Hard Forest.

At first, I was thrilled. The barracks—with their hot showers and dry beds—were within sight. It was November, and the air was chilly, but manageable. Then, on the first morning, the sky broke.

It started as a cold, needles-and-pins November rain. We had our wet-weather gear and field jackets, but the rain was relentless. It did not just fall; it saturated. It rained for five straight days. Everything we owned was soaked to the core. Our leather boots became heavy sponges; our socks, underwear, rucksacks, and even our toiletries were dripping. And the psychological kicker? The drill sergeants would not allow us to cross that narrow strip of asphalt to the barracks to get dry gear. We had to live in the rot.

We were miserable, huddled in fighting positions we had dug into the mud, pulling guard duty while water pooled in our boots. But on the fifth day, things took a turn for the worse. The temperature plunged, and the rain turned to sleet. Within minutes, the temperature dropped below freezing, and ice began to glaze our soaked uniforms.

We received the order to pack up. The collective sigh of relief was audible; we were sure we were heading back to the comfort of our barracks for a much-needed hot shower and meal. Our rucksacks, once 50 pounds, now felt like 70 because the wool and nylon were heavy with water. We lined up in two columns, the smell of the chow hall wafting across the street like a cruel joke. We had been eating MREs (Meals Ready to Eat) for a week, and the thought of a hot tray was the only thing keeping us upright.

Instead of turning toward the barracks, we turned toward the motor pool. I was confused and freezing. We marched into a maintenance bay where space heaters were roaring, blowing warm air that felt like a gift from heaven. We grounded our rucks, tore into MREs, and waited. I saw the drill sergeants—who were just as wet and exhausted as we were—huddled together, shaking their heads in disbelief.

One of them came over and broke the news. The rain had successfully extinguished the forest fires in the original training area. The Squadron Commander, wanting to ensure we were "combat ready," decided we would still do the full 20–30-mile road march.

I honestly felt like I was in a bad dream. It was there, in that motor pool bay, that I learned a skill I use to this day: the ability to go somewhere else in my mind. I learned to dissociate from the pain, the cold, and the misery. I retreated into a safe place inside my head. We lined up and marched out of that warm bay directly into a full-blown winter storm. The sleet had turned to blinding snow. Visibility was down to 50 feet.

We marched for hours that felt like lifetimes. We were not just carrying rucksacks; we were burdened by the full weight of our "steel pots" (helmets), web gear loaded down with canteens and ammo pouches, and our rifles. The gloves we had been issued—leather shells with wool inserts—were a cruel joke. They had become soaked through and frozen solid, doing little more than shielding our skin from the direct bite of the freezing wind. It was, without question, the most physically and mentally miserable I have ever been.

I trudged on, my mind eventually checking out as a survival mechanism. I focused entirely on the man in front of me, managing to stay just close enough to keep his silhouette in sight through the blinding, blowing snow. My world had shrunk down to the few feet of white powder directly in front of my boots.

Shells of Men

Somehow, through sheer muscle memory and grit, we reached our destination sometime the next morning. We were no longer a unit of vibrant soldiers; we were mere shells of human beings. With fingers numb and frozen stiff, we struggled to set up our shelters in the deep snow. Once the canvas was up, we collapsed, sleeping the heavy, dreamless sleep of the dead.

We were eventually roused when the Commander drove out in the comfort of his warm vehicle to tell us how "proud" he was of our performance. The irony was not lost on us, but the resentment was dulled by exhaustion. Thankfully, we were told we would be trucked back the following day rather than having to march.

We ate a semi-hot meal served from mermite cans—the heat barely reaching our core—before heading back to sleep early. Yet, even in our shattered state, the mission continued; we still managed to pull our weight, rotating through fire guard and perimeter duty throughout the night.

· · ·

The Long Road Back

The next morning, the hope that had sustained us evaporated: the trucks never came. Instead, the First Sergeant arrived, his presence a harbinger of the news we all dreaded. The transportation had been canceled. There would be no ride back to the warmth of the barracks; we were road-marching the entire way back.

I wanted to quit. The feeling was a physical weight, heavier than the rucksack on my back. I was not alone in that despair; I heard others give voice to it—grown men sobbing in the snow, their spirits finally broken by the unrelenting cold. To survive, I retreated once again. I checked out of the physical world and fled to that safe, quiet place deep within my mind.

A Surreal Sight

At some point during that grueling trek back, a deer suddenly appeared, darting with effortless grace through our two columns of marching men. I watched it disappear into the trees and a single, desperate thought flickered through my mind: *"run away... You are so lucky. I want to run away with you."* It was a strange, fleeting wish that spoke volumes about the fractured state of my mind at that point in the journey.

Beyond that encounter, the rest of the march is a blurred haze of exhaustion and ice. My next clear memory is the surreal, almost cinematic sight of our arrival at Squadron Headquarters. There stood the Commander—dry, warm, and obviously well-rested. He had military music blaring and stood at a rigid salute as we limped past him, a parade of the broken and the frozen.

Somehow, through a sheer act of will that defies logic, we had road-marched close to 60 miles in a mere day and a half, navigating through a gauntlet of ice and snow. We had survived the impossible, though at a cost only those in those columns would ever understand.

When we finally reached the barracks, men simply collapsed where they stood. My legs were locking up, my muscles spasming from the cold and the weight. I later found out from a drill sergeant that there had been 10 cases of exhaustion, 4 cases of immersion foot, and 4 cases of frostbite. Ten people were taken away by ambulance, including two drill sergeants. There were rumors that the Commander was relieved for trainee abuse, but I never cared about the politics. I only cared that I had survived.

The experience of basic training left me with a new "gear" I did not realize I had. Before Fort Knox, I never imagined I could endure something so grueling and cross the finish line. By the end, I was perpetually sore and exhausted, yet deeply proud. My fellow scouts and I had bonded throughout the course, but it was the "Freezing Field-Week" that truly cemented us as lifelong brothers. We had navigated the highs and lows of training together, and we emerged on the other side as finely tuned fighting machines. We had shared laughs and shed tears on many occasions, forming a bond that only shared suffering can create.

While the pain and suffering were constant companions in one form or another, there were also more than enough moments of humor to last a lifetime. One such incident occurred during the day and night live-fire courses—a transition I always wanted to make from one world to another.

I will never forget one evening while we were huddled together, waiting for the sun to dip below the horizon. We were preparing for the night fire range—the infamous course where you must crawl through the mud and dirt while a ceiling of live rounds and glowing tracers' streaks just feet above your head. As we sat in the grass eating our MREs, the boredom led to a dangerous level of bravado. We started joking around, whispering about how one of our Drill Sergeants looked exactly like Jimmy Walker, who played J.J. on the hit show *Good Times*. We were laughing hysterically, lost in the imitation, completely unaware that another Drill Sergeant was standing just within earshot, absorbing every word.

A "DY-NO-MITE" Night

We successfully navigated the chaos of the night-fire course, and by the next morning, we were back at the rifle range to continue our marksmanship training. I was positioned down in my firing pit, my cheek pressed against the stock of my rifle, and my eyes focused intently on the target downrange. Suddenly, I felt a sharp, **"TAP, TAP, TAP"** on my steel pot helmet.

I looked up, and my heart instantly sank into my stomach. Standing above me was the very Drill Sergeant who bore the resemblance to J.J., staring down at me with a cold, unreadable expression that signaled immediate trouble.

"Yes, Drill Sergeant?" I stammered, my voice cracking slightly.

He did not yell. He just glared at me with a terrifyingly calm intensity. "Elvis, I heard you think I look like someone," he said, his voice dropping an octave. Then, leaning in, he added, "Well, tonight, you and I are going to have a **DY-NO-MITE** time!"

True to his word, that night I was certain I performed more push-ups and mountain climbers than any other soldier in the history of the United States Army. I was thoroughly thrashed, every muscle screaming in protest as I eventually limped off to start my guard duty shift.

The funny thing is, after that incident, our relationship changed. We grew closer. Instead of just being another face in the platoon, I was on his radar. He began picking me for the "good" details, and on the nights when I had fire guard, he would often sit and talk with me. He shared his wisdom about what to truly expect as a scout, teaching me how to prepare for the field and handle the specific challenges of 19 Delta life. It was a transition from raw discipline to genuine mentorship, proving that even in the toughest environments, respect is often earned through a mix of grit and a little bit of shared trouble.

Torchlight Inauguration

After enduring the grueling physical toll of the "Three Sisters," the suffocating humidity of Kentucky, the relentless discipline of the drill sergeants, and the hell of field week, I finally reached the moment I had fought so hard for. I had navigated every high peak and low valley, and the pride I felt as I prepared to graduate as a scout was unlike anything I had ever experienced. I felt God beside me every step of the way, but still did not put him first.

Our graduation ceremony was not a standard parade-ground affair; it was a rite of passage held under the flickering glow of torchlight in the dead of night. We stood in formation, our faces still smeared with dark camouflage paint, clad in full combat gear as if ready to deploy at a moment's notice. The shadows cast by the torches danced across the ranks, adding a sense of ancient gravity to the occasion.

As the ceremony progressed, we were formally inducted into a lineage that stretched back through the centuries. Our names were added to the historical rolls of the Cavalry—a roster that included legendary figures like Ronald Reagan, Teddy Roosevelt, George Custer, Wild Bill Hickok, Kit Carson, and Buffalo Bill. Standing there in the cool night air, I realized the magnitude of what I had achieved. I had earned my Stetson. I had earned my place. Our commander handed us our RECON patch and saluted each one of us.

I scanned the sea of parents and family members who had traveled to support their scouts, watching the bittersweet, much-needed reunions unfolding after sixteen weeks away from home. I found myself half-expecting to see a familiar face in the crowd, but deep inside, a quiet voice reminded me that no one was there for me. I understood the reality of it; the high cost of travel and the unrelenting day-to-day struggle of work and life meant those closest to me had to remain at home.

Rather than dwelling on the void, I stepped forward and volunteered for whatever tasks needed to be done. I wanted to clear the way so my battle-buddies could cherish every possible second with their families.

Though I stood alone in that moment, I stood with a swelling sense of pride. I was no longer that sickly boy from Lawton—the one people whispered about, doubting he would ever see his twelfth birthday. I had defied the odds, outrun the doctors' grim predictions, and outlasted the United States Army's toughest trials.

I had been forged into something new. I was a 19 Delta. I was a Cavalryman. I was a scout.

9

DEATH VALLEY

After graduation, I was able to go home for a few days to visit some of my family. I did not have much time, but the visit was jarring; it made me realize how much my perspective had shifted. Everything looked different through the eyes of a soldier. My civilian clothes no longer fit—I had physically outgrown my old life—and I felt a strange void when I was not running every day or eating my three meals at the exact, regimented times the Army dictated. I was a different person now, finally stepping into my role as a protector with a hard-earned sense of accomplishment. At that time, God was still on my "back burner"—someone I kept in reserve for emergencies only—but He was undeniably there, waiting in the wings of my life.

My orders were for Fort Irwin, California—situated deep in the heart of the Mojave Desert. If Kentucky had been a wooded, humid forest that hid its secrets in the brush, Fort Irwin was a stark, unforgiving moonscape. It was a land defined by volcanic rocks, shimmering heat waves that distorted the horizon, and the twisted, haunting silhouettes of Joshua trees.

It was here, in the "National Training Center" (NTC), that my "emergency contact" relationship with God was forced to change. In the vast, lonely expanse of the desert, there is no noise to drown out the spirit and nowhere to hide from yourself—or from the Creator. The desert has a way of stripping away your pretenses and leaving you with nothing but your character and your need for something greater than your own strength. Amidst the dust and the silence of the high desert, the "protector" began to realize that even he needed a Shield.

The Crucible of the High Desert

Life at the National Training Center (NTC) was a grueling, daily lesson in endurance. It served as a constant reminder of just how vital realistic training is for any combat unit or individual soldier. NTC is **the** premier desert training facility for the United States Army, the place where every stateside combat unit eventually rotates to be forged in the heat of desert warfare.

Units rotating through the National Training Center (NTC) at Fort Irwin, CA, primarily encounter two phases of training: Force-on-Force operations and Live-Fire exercises. These phases, conducted in the Mojave Desert, are designed to simulate Large-Scale Combat Operations against an adversary, over approximately 14 to 21 days.

I was assigned to the Live Fire phase, where the environment was as real as it gets. On many occasions, I learned exactly what it sounded like to be in the middle of the chaos—the sharp, metallic ring of shrapnel and the distinct crack of small-arms fire hitting my M551 Sheridan tank we used as armored Taxis.

The lessons the Army units absorbed in that sand and wind went a long way in preparing them for the desert warfare that lay on the horizon. I remained there for 21 straight rotations, and while I gained a mastery of combat tactics, I also received several harsh lessons in just how fragile life truly is.

. . .

The Weight of the Inadequate

One life-changing incident occurred involving a young woman I had met in Barstow, the town closest to the base. One evening, she and her boyfriend came over to our house, driven by a sudden and deep-seated need to ask questions about God. They had both been raised in the Catholic faith, but they confessed that they felt they did not really *know* Him on a personal level.

I sat with them and shared everything I could remember from my Sunday school classes, Church Sermons, and my mother's faithful teachings. Even as I spoke, I felt a gnawing sense of inadequacy; I was a soldier, not a preacher, and my words were clumsy. I talked for a while, offering what comfort and knowledge I had. Eventually, they said their goodbyes and left, and I went to bed, thinking I would see them again soon.

The next day, the world shattered. I found out that moments after leaving the house, they were involved in a horrific automobile accident. She had been killed instantly.

The realization hit me with the force of a physical blow. The "inadequate" conversation we had just hours before was the last chance she ever had to hear about the Lord. It was a sobering reminder that we are never guaranteed a "next time" to say what needs to be said.

The weight of that news crushed me. I felt a paralyzing sense of guilt and remorse because I had not known enough of the Gospel to share it clearly. I felt like I had failed her in her final hour. Fear began to seep in. I remember a voice in my head—I know now it was not God, but the enemy—whispering, "You are next." Less than a month later, it nearly happened.

The Wreckage in the Desert

In early November 1988, on the lonely, windswept road that stretches from Fort Irwin toward Barstow, my life as I knew it ended. A friend of mine had offered to drive me into Barstow so we could do some looking around and shopping, a much-needed reprieve since we had just returned from six grueling days in the field.

I was sitting in the passenger seat of that small Toyota truck, exhausted from the field. I had tucked my seatbelt shoulder strap behind my back and leaned into the passenger window, hoping to catch a nap during the 45-minute desert trip. About halfway through the drive, where the flat desert floor begins to rise into treacherous hills and sharp curves, my friend tried to pass another vehicle while traveling over 100 mph around a bend.

We lost control instantly, and the world dissolved into a blur. The vehicle did not just lose its grip on the pavement or succumb to a simple slide. Instead, it launched, propelled by its own violent momentum into the thin, biting cold of the desert air. For a few terrifying seconds, gravity ceased to exist, replaced by the sickening weightlessness of a high-speed trajectory as the world began to spin in a sequence of destruction.

Then came the impact. The truck did not just crash; it began a series of white-hot, bone-shattering rolls across the jagged Mojave terrain. Every rotation was a symphony of twisting metal and shattering glass —the "tiny diamonds" of safety glass I would come to know so well— as the desert floor rose up repeatedly to meet us. In those chaotic moments, I was completely defenseless, tossed like a ragdoll in a cage of steel.

This was the "emergency" I had kept God in reserve for, but as the truck tumbled through the darkness, I was not just reaching for a back-burner faith; I was hitting the limits of my own mortality. The desert that had been a moonscape of rocks suddenly became the altar where my old life was broken apart so that something new could eventually be built from the wreckage.

One. Two. Three. The familiar, grounded landscape of the High Desert vanished, replaced by a terrifying kaleidoscope of shattering glass and the high-pitched, agonizing screech of twisting steel. The centrifugal force was absolute—a swirling chaos that defied the laws of gravity.

Four. Five. Six. Seven. Seven times, the car flipped end over end—a brutal assault of physics against metal and bone. In the Bible, seven is the number of completion—the mark of a finished work. By every physical law known to man, my life should have been "completed" right there in the dirt. The math was simple: a crash of that magnitude, occurring in such total isolation, should have resulted in a closed book.

But as the dust settled and the heavy silence returned to the desert, it became clear that while the vehicle was finished, I was not. My story was not ending; it was being rewritten in the wreckage. I had been shattered, but the very "Emergency Contact" I had kept at a distance was the only reason my heart was still beating amidst the twisted remains of that Toyota.

Assessing the Damage

The world had been a violent blur of motion. I remember the jarring impact of my head slamming hard into the dashboard as the truck began its journey down the road, punctuated by the sickening, metallic crunch of the roof caving in with every rotation. When the wreckage finally groaned to a halt, the truck lay upside down, having rolled down the steep embankment on the side of the road.

In the middle of that empty desert, the silence that followed was deafening. I found myself lying half-in and half-out of the shattered passenger window. I was on my back, staring straight up into the vast, deep, star-filled sky. I managed to scoot myself out of the wreckage about 5 feet before I felt a deep, dull pain in my abdomen.

The night air was biting, and despite my thick jacket, I began to shiver uncontrollably. These were not just small chills; they were violent tremors that I could not suppress. In my daze, a single question repeated in my mind: *Why am I shaking?* I did not yet understand that my body was in shock, struggling to process the trauma.

My vision was clouded as blood, warm and thick, began to seep into my eyes from the impact. I had hit the dashboard with such tremendous force that I did not just see the typical "stars"; I saw vivid, three-dimensional constellations. They had an immense, infinite depth to them, swirling and dancing in the dark like a private galaxy within my own mind.

A strange, detached logic—a psychological insulation—took over. I remember thinking quite calmly, as if I were a bystander watching someone else's disaster: *"That's going to hurt later."* In that moment, suspended between the wreckage and the stars, I was a man waiting to see what the next chapter of a supposedly "completed" life would look like.

As I lay there on the cold, indifferent sand, a heavy, sour smell began to fill my nostrils. It was overwhelming and pungent, seeming to saturate the very air around me, but my clouded, shock-ridden mind could not identify it. I was drenched in the fluid, yet in the terrifying chaos of the moment, I could not place the scent. It was only much later that the gruesome pieces of the puzzle came together: as the truck had flipped end-over-end those seven times, the battery had exploded under the hood, and I had been sprayed and covered in caustic battery acid.

Seeking any small reprieve from the rising tide of agony, I instinctively pulled my feet back toward me, so my knees were arched up. The moment I changed position, I felt a slight, instant relief in my abdomen. Even through the fog of trauma, I knew something was deeply wrong inside.

The memory of the impact was a blur, but I could just barely recall the sensation of being thrown violently forward with the force of a hundred-mile-per-hour stop. Because I had tucked the shoulder strap behind me to nap, the seatbelt had acted like a blunt-force guillotine, stopping me suddenly and exclusively around my waist. The lap belt had held me in the seat, but it had also focused the entire kinetic energy of the crash into my midsection, allowing my internal organs to slam to a stop.

As the desert silence pressed in, I was a "Scout" in a different kind of reconnaissance—trying to survey the damage of my own broken body. I had the sense to move my hands and feet, and I was thankful I could. I was a protector who could not move or speak, a soldier caught in a chemical wash of acid and blood. In that moment, I prayed quietly in my mind, waiting on the sand for a miracle I was not even sure I had the right to ask for.

The driver, through some miracle, had managed to hold onto the steering wheel throughout the entire accident; he walked away with nothing more than a bruised elbow. I remember watching him through the haze as he wandered aimlessly around the wreckage in the dark. He was completely dazed, his voice echoing in the desert as he lamented repeatedly, "My truck... look at my truck."

He eventually found me and asked if I was okay. I could not respond. The pain in my head and abdomen was a white-hot roar. The desert night had a strange, blue tint. Then, the world went black.

Life in the Balance

Fort Irwin is 45 minutes from Barstow. The road between them is a narrow ribbon of asphalt littered with crosses—memorials to the many soldiers who have died on that stretch. It lulls you into a false sense of security, leading you to go too fast, until it takes everything from you. The 15-foot embankment that the truck had rolled down was completely hidden from the road. If someone had not seen the dust cloud or the flicker of our lights, I would have internally bled out in the dark.

But someone saw. Through the darkness of that lonely desert road, headlights slowed and pulled to the shoulder. A car stopped, and then another, the sound of slamming doors echoing down the embankment.

I began to drift in and out of consciousness, my reality flickering like a dying bulb. I remember a moment of clarity where I saw three figures standing over me, their silhouettes framed against the vast, star-filled sky. When I slipped away and then surged back to the surface of consciousness again, that small group had grown; now, there were about ten people surrounding me, a wall of faces staring down at me.

The night air was still biting, and the cold had settled deep into my bones. I heard a distant, urgent voice command: "Put your coats on him." Suddenly, I felt a heavy, comforting weight as several jackets were piled onto my broken body, a makeshift barrier against the desert chill.

Once more, the world went dark. When I came back again, the scene had shifted. I saw a medic hovering over me, the sharp glint of trauma shears in his hand. He began cutting through the sleeve of my brand-new Levi's quilted jacket—a piece of clothing I was proud of. Even in my shattered state, a flash of protest flared in my mind. I remember thinking with a strange, lucid stubbornness, " Don't *cut it... just take it off,* before the darkness pulled me under once more, and I slipped away again.

I woke up as they were running up the embankment with me on a spine board. I heard a medic shout, "His blood pressure is 80 over 60 and dropping, we have to hurry!" Every bounce of the board sent searing agony through my stomach. I woke up one last time in the back of an ambulance, hearing the driver yell "Bumps!" as we sped toward the hospital, the jolts causing me to black out from the sheer intensity of the pain.

As I lay in that ambulance, God was already at work. While my breath had flickered out, the prayers back in Lawton hadn't stopped. My mother nightly was standing in the spiritual gap, just as she had stood in the red mud of the tornado.

There was a logistical battle happening behind the scenes. Because the accident was closer to Barstow, I should have gone there. But Barstow EMS and Fort Irwin were having a jurisdictional dispute. Barstow refused to send an ambulance, saying I was a "soldier" and therefore Fort Irwin's problem. It took the Irwin ambulance 35 minutes to reach me and 35 minutes to get back—precious time I did not have. But God's timing is perfect even when men are petty.

Fort Irwin had just added a surgeon to their staff at Weed Army Hospital. Major James Woodham was the man who saved my life. Something else amazing happened that I found out later. My brother Billy had called, trying to tell me about a dream he had, but could not reach me because I was in the hospital after the accident. He had a dream in which I was lying on the side of the road, and an Angel picked me up and carried me to safety. He saw the Angels that God dispatched to protect me.

I was taught in Sunday school about Shadrach, Meshach, and Abednego in the Bible who were forced into a furnace for not worshipping another King. The furnace was heated seven times hotter than usual—a "complete" fire meant to ensure destruction. Yet they walked out without the smell of smoke because a Fourth Man was with them. In that crumpled car, after the seventh roll, the Fourth Man was there. My large intestine had been punctured, leaking toxins into my system. I was septic and dying, and during surgery, my heart stopped three times, but I was able to come back each time due to the team God had assembled, well ahead of time.

I woke up after surgery with a realization: I was a scout who had lost his way, but I had been found by the only One who could lead me home. I could not treat God like a 911 operator anymore. I had been dodging Him to please myself, but He had just pulled me out of the grave.

Healing and New Beginnings

I spent the next several months focused entirely on the arduous process of recovery, working to heal from my injuries while serving out the rest of my time in the arid, unforgiving expanse of the Mojave Desert. The progress was slow and measured in inches. I had to relearn the basic mechanics of movement, working painstakingly to sit up and eventually stand properly.

My body had been a map of the accident; the surgeons had been forced to open my abdomen to repair my large intestine, which had been severely compromised by the blunt force of the seatbelt. I was left with 52 surgical staples running up my stomach—a silver ladder of scars that eventually made for a good conversation starter.

Despite the trauma, the "Scout" in me refused to stay down. I started lifting weights, pushing through the pulling sensation of the scar tissue, trying to reclaim my strength and get back into top condition so I could continue my journey. By that point, I had been in the Army for less than two years on an original two-year enlistment. Most people would have taken the exit, but despite the physical toll the desert and my injuries had taken, my commitment to the service had not wavered. I did not just stay; I doubled down and decided to re-enlist for four more years. That decision opened a door I had not expected: the opportunity to return to my roots in Lawton.

Heading East

In the military's strategic layout, Fort Sill was primarily known as a major field artillery base. However, even an artillery stronghold requires specific support units to function effectively—specifically, one infantry battalion and one scout platoon to act as the "eyes and ears" on the ground.

It felt like more than just a coincidence or a savvy career move. After being broken open in the Mojave and stitched back together, I was being sent back to the red dirt that first formed me. I was not just returning to Oklahoma; I was returning with a renewed strength and a specific mission, ready to serve the land of my "Sunday school" memories with the discipline of a man who had survived the fire. I was stepping back onto familiar ground, as if a circle was finally closing. Upon arriving at Fort Sill, I began a new chapter in leadership and took on the role of an instructor. I was responsible for shaping the next generation of leadership, teaching incoming officers the intricate, high-stakes art of calling for fire along with essential basic combat techniques.

It was a position of great responsibility—taking everything I had learned in the dust of the Mojave and the trials of training and passing it on to those who would soon lead men into the field.

While there, my life took a personal turn when I was reacquainted with a dear friend from my junior high and high school days. We had always shared a deep connection, with laughter serving as our common language. Our bond deepened quickly; after a year of dating, we were married.

Ten months later, our first son was born. I was absolutely elated. More than anything, I had wanted a son—someone to play with and a chance to finally be the father I never had. I remember his first night home vividly; I stayed up until dawn, simply watching him sleep in his crib. I found myself constantly checking whether he was still breathing, as the gentle rise and fall of his tiny chest was almost imperceptible to the eye.

At that moment, it felt as though I had the world at my fingertips. I had just been promoted to Sergeant, and I had a beautiful new son to boot. Being back on Oklahoma soil felt like a well-deserved peace, but it was destined to be short-lived. Just two months after my son was born, the military called again. I received new orders for Germany, where I was to be assigned to the 4th Squadron, 7th Cavalry, 3rd Armored Division.

10

GERMANY AND BEYOND

We had been married for only a year and a half, and our first son was just two months old when we moved our young family to Germany. It was a season of dizzying transitions; we were just beginning to weave the fabric of our lives together, navigating the exhaustion and complexities of new parenthood while being simultaneously uprooted and replanted in a foreign land.

Even though we had only been in-country for a few months, we had already fallen deeply in love with the local culture. We found solace and peace in traditional German *Gasthauses*. These local taverns became our weekly eatery, where we would retreat to enjoy the rich, hearty food that nourished the soul as much as the body. Inside, the fireplaces glowed with a deep, inviting warmth that stood in stark contrast to the biting, relentless cold of the German winter howling outside the thick stone walls.

The quaint little towns surrounding the base felt cozy and welcoming, as did the locals. We quickly learned that a little effort went a long way; the people showed a genuine appreciation whenever we tried to speak their language, meeting our broken German with kindness. One such town was Lorbach, a place that became a scenic part of my soldiering life. Every morning, we would leave the gates of our *kaserne*—our military base—and run our PT. I can still hear the synchronized sound of our combat boots echoing off the cobblestones as we ran right down into the very heart of the town, the morning mist clinging to the narrow streets.

Living there felt less like a standard military assignment and more like an immersion into a world that embraced us. It was a beautiful, quiet interval in our lives, even as we lived thousands of miles away from the red dirt of Oklahoma and everything we had ever known. In those moments, breathing in the crisp air of Lorbach, I felt that inheritance—a brief, peaceful harbor before the winds of war began to blow.

The Beauty of Germany

The cobblestone streets and the ancient, looming fortress of Büdingen, Germany, offered a comforting embrace, serving as a dream come true for a history lover like me. There was a hushed, timeless quality to the architecture that made our presence feel like a small, fleeting chapter in a much larger, enduring story—a brief whisper against the backdrop of centuries. Driven by this sense of wonder, we traversed Germany as extensively as possible, intent on visiting every castle we could find. We found ourselves captivated by a landscape where the sheer beauty was consistently breathtaking: emerald-green rolling hills gave way to dense, fairytale forests, and every river bend seemed to reveal a crumbling ruin or a perfectly preserved spire reaching toward the clouds.

The experience was a rich sensory tapestry that pulled me in from every direction. I found myself mesmerized by the distinct, intricate geometry of the timber-framed houses, their chestnut oak beams carving patterns against white plaster like a structural puzzle. In the town squares, the lively sounds of daily life breathed movement into the ancient stones. It was a place where tradition felt alive, often punctuated by locals in authentic lederhosen and dirndls, their attire a proud nod to a heritage that refused to fade.

These moments were deeply grounded in the incredible food and drink that made the culture feel even more welcoming. We spent afternoons tucked into wood-paneled taverns, where the air was thick with the savory aroma of sizzling schnitzel, hearty bratwurst, and warm, salty pretzels. The hospitality was often served in heavy, ornate beer steins, their pewter lids clicking shut after every cool, crisp sip of local lager. This combination of grand history and warm, tangible hospitality turned every meal into a celebration, making the vast German landscape feel, for a moment, like home.

The Jack-of-all-Trades

The unique hallmark of being a Cavalry Scout in the United States Army is the sheer variety of combat platforms you must master. Depending on your unit and mission, you can be assigned to a Bradley Fighting Vehicle, a helicopter, an M113, a motorcycle, or a Humvee; you might be a dismounted "ground-pounder" or, in later years, part of a Stryker crew. Being a scout is a multifaceted job that demands a wide range of skills, and I was about to receive a high-stakes crash course in the Bradley Fighting Vehicle (BFV).

Up until this pivotal junction in my career, my experience in the Cavalry had been diverse and rugged. I had served as a dismounted scout, operating on the ground with nothing but my pack and my wits, and I had commanded or operated a variety of vehicles: M113 Armored Personnel Carriers, Humvees, and even the nimble but aging M551 Sheridan tanks. However, there was one glaring hole in my resume: I had never once set foot on an M3 Bradley Fighting Vehicle.

To serve effectively in this new Bradley heavy unit, I needed to be qualified on the BFV platform, but time was a luxury the geopolitical climate simply would not afford me. I arrived in

Germany in October 1990, stepping into a world that was bracing for impact. As soon as the ink on my in-processing paperwork was dry, our unit received its formal mission orders to move to the Middle East.

Because I was a Non-Commissioned Officer (NCO), the Army granted me the autonomy to handle my in-processing appointments without supervision. I was a twenty-one-year-old Sergeant, seasoned by my training but still young in the grand scheme of life. Assigned to the same unit alongside me was a Private First Class named Charles Scott Walker. At nineteen, Walker was just a kid, though he did not necessarily act like one. He had a brother in the military and arrived with a solid grasp of Army life and a clear understanding of his responsibilities.

Since we were both arriving in the unit at the same time, I was tasked with ensuring Walker navigated the maze of in-processing and had all the gear he needed. We spent those first few weeks getting to know each other. Because Walker lived in the barracks and I lived off-post, my wife and I would occasionally have him and other soldiers over for a home-cooked dinner—a small slice of normalcy before the storm.

The Responsibility of Command

Once in-processing was complete, the Army's formal structure took over, with its rigid hierarchies and clear lines of authority. In a turn of fate that would define the coming years, we were both assigned to the same troop and the same platoon. Walker was now officially my soldier. This was not just a title; as his first-line supervisor, I became his mentor, his disciplinarian, and the man responsible for his life and well-being.

The buildup for deployment was relentless and unforgiving. We hit the ground running, laboring through the frantic, high-stakes preparations needed to move an entire armored unit and all its heavy equipment across the globe. We spent long hours in the motor pools and in the field, readying the vehicles and the men for the unknown.

Honestly, in those early days, our bond was born of necessity; we only really knew each other because we were both "new guys"—outsiders in a unit comprised of established soldiers who had already formed their own tight-knit circles. We were the "new blood" trying to find our footing while the world shifted beneath us.

Though the military command kept the specifics close to the chest and we did not have an exact departure date, the atmosphere in Germany had changed. The air was thick with a heavy, undeniable realization that reached into every barracks room and motor pool: the "Long Walk" was coming. The time for training was over, and we would be leaving for the theater of war very soon.

We could feel the season of peace slipping away, replaced by the cold machinery of mobilization. I looked at Walker and the rest of my squad, knowing that the "gap" I was called to stand in was no longer a metaphor—it was about to become a physical reality in the sands of the Middle East.

My Steel Horse

I spent every waking moment in a state of intellectual combat, cramming the intricacies of the Bradley Fighting Vehicle into my mind as quickly as humanly possible. Because I held the rank of Sergeant but was still a "rookie" on this specific platform, the commander appointed me as the Senior Dismount. Walker, a Private First Class, was assigned as a scout on my specific BFV. This appointment made me the leader for any dismounted operations we would conduct. When the ramp dropped in a combat zone, the mission was on my shoulders.

The M3 BFV is the specialized Cavalry version of the Bradley, and it is a different beast entirely from the infantry's M2. While the M2 is designed to carry a squad of troops, the M3 is configured for maximum reconnaissance lethality. It sacrifices troop space for an arsenal of extra ammunition and high-tech surveillance equipment.

The vehicle is run by a core crew of three: the driver tucked in the hull, and the gunner and commander situated in the turret. In the rear—the back compartment—there is space for one to three observers. In the dry humor of the Cavalry, these men were affectionately and irreverently known as "JAFOs" (Just Another F'ing Observer). My primary role was to lead these JAFOs out of the belly of the beast and into the unpredictable "sand dunes." We were the unit's dismounted eyes and ears, leaving the safety of the armor to conduct boots-on-the-ground reconnaissance. However, in the fluid, high-tempo environment of a scout platoon, roles were never static; cross-training was survival. I eventually stepped into the gunner's seat and the commander's hatch whenever the situation demanded it.

I was as prepared as I was ever going to be as we watched the massive, armored silhouettes of our Bradleys being winched and secured onto flatbed railcars. They were destined for a port where they would be swallowed by massive transport ships bound for the desert sands of Saudi Arabia. The scale of the machinery was immense, but it paled in comparison to the personal cost of this deployment.

Historic Sabers

We were the "Spearhead" of the 3rd Armored Division, deployed initially for the defensive buildup of Operation Desert Shield and, eventually, for the lightning-strike offensive of Operation Desert Storm. Our unit, the 4th Squadron, 7th Cavalry, was steeped in a history so rich and storied that you could feel the weight of it every time you donned your Stetson or looked at the crossed sabers on your uniform. The 7th Cavalry was not just a unit; it was a lineage of warriors who had seen the harshest winters and the most desperate battles of days past.

The most infamous chapter of this history belonged to the 7th Cavalry under George Armstrong Custer at the Battle of the Little Bighorn. That spirit of being the first ones in—the scouts who find the enemy and hold the line—stayed the cornerstone of our identity.

More recently, the 7th Cavalry etched its name in the annals of modern warfare at Landing Zone X-Ray in the Ia Drang Valley of Vietnam. This was the first major air-mobile battle in history, where the "Garry Owen" troopers proved their mettle against overwhelming odds. This battle was immortalized in the seminal book *We Were Soldiers Once... and Young,* by Lt. Gen. Harold G. Moore and Joseph L. Galloway, which was later adapted into the movie, *We Were Soldiers* starring Mel Gibson.

In the Army, military history is far more than just a collection of dates and names in a textbook; it is a vital part of your professional development. When you stand before a promotion board, you are not just tested on your tactical ability; you are grilled on the specific instances of your unit's history. You are expected to know whose boots you are filling.

The 7th Cavalry has a long and venerated history, and as we sat in the Saudi Arabian sand, we were acutely aware of the ghosts of the troopers who had come before us. I did not know it at the time, but the "Spearhead" was about to be thrust into the heat of battle once again. We were not just students of history anymore; we were on the verge of writing our own chapter in the history books, adding the dust of the Middle East to the legends of the 7th Cavalry.

The Weight of Departure

As our departure date loomed, I was struck by a heavy sense of longing. I looked at the vibrant beauty surrounding my young family —the peace and history we had momentarily called home—and wished, with everything in me, that I did not have to leave it all behind. The warmth of the German countryside stood in stark, painful contrast to the cold uncertainty of the war that awaited us.

Now, with a son only four months old, I had to go. On Christmas Eve 1990, while the rest of the world was singing carols and opening gifts, I stood in three feet of biting German snow and boarded a C-130 transport plane. As the engines roared to life, I was leaving behind the frozen winter and my young family, heading toward the scorching, unknown heat of the desert. The transition was jarring—not just in temperature, but in the realization that the training was over and the "Long Walk" had truly begun.

11

CULTURE SHOCK

Within a matter of mere months, my world had undergone a staggering series of transformations that left the "Scout" in me constantly recalibrating. I had been uprooted from the familiar, solid red dirt of Oklahoma and transplanted into the silent, snow-covered pine forests of Germany. Then, before I could even adjust to the European winter, I was sent into the shifting, endless sands of the Middle East. The sheer speed of these transitions was enough to give a man emotional whiplash.

The desert at night is the loneliest place on Earth. It is a vast, echoing void where the horizon disappears into an ink-black sky, leaving you with nothing but your thoughts and the stars. Before our heavy equipment arrived, we were driven deep into the heart of the Saudi Arabian interior—the "Empty Quarter"—to await the arrival of our Bradley Fighting Vehicles from the port.

There was absolutely nothing there but us. No landmarks, no buildings, no signs of civilization—just a small band of cavalry troopers in an ocean of dunes. It was a desolate, punishing environment where the wind blew continually, a relentless force that had its own personality. That wind was an invasive enemy. It drove fine, powdery sand into every imaginable crack and crevice. It found its way into the delicate internal components of our equipment, the seals of our containers, and eventually, into our very skin. You ate the sand, you breathed the sand, and you slept in the sand. It was a constant, abrasive reminder that we were no longer in control of our surroundings; we were guests in a landscape that did not particularly want us there. We were scouts waiting for our "Steel Horses" to arrive, sitting in a silence so thick it felt heavy.

The First Mission: Tracers and Trials

January 17, 1991, is a date forever etched in my memory. In the Army, the rhythm of your life is dictated by the sun; you must always be in your fighting positions, fully combat-ready, before the sun rises and before it sets. This protocol, known as "stand to," is a disciplined ritual that ensures you are not caught off guard during the "danger times"—those dawn and dusk windows when an enemy is most likely to launch an assault.

During "stand to" on that cold January morning, Operation Desert Shield officially kicked off. Since our Bradleys had not yet arrived at our forward position, we had dug deep fighting positions into the sand to man in case we were needed to defend the line.

Through the thick, pre-dawn darkness, we watched a spectacle of raw power. Massive bombers flew incredibly low over our positions, almost skimming the desert floor to evade radar before pulling into steep, aggressive climbs to begin their bombing runs into Iraq.

The silence of the desert gave way to a bone-deep vibration. The ground beneath our boots rumbled with the constant, distant thunder of heavy explosions echoing from across the border. This was not just the beginning of combat operations for the Coalition; for me, it was the pivotal day I received my very first reconnaissance mission of the war. The "Eyes and Ears" were finally being sent out to work.

The Aerial Recon Mission

Our troop's vehicles were still being processed and offloaded at the Port of Dammam, so we were living in the transient uncertainty of tents in the sand. My Troop Commander (CO), Captain Jeff Hicks—a man for whom I felt an instant admiration and still hold in the highest respect—approached me with our first reconnaissance mission.

He ordered me to select two other scouts and report at once to the Squadron Commander (SCO), Lieutenant Colonel Terry Tucker. Without hesitation, I chose two men I knew I could rely on in a tight spot: PFC Gary Nielsen and my young shadow, PFC Walker. We gathered our gear and moved with a sense of purpose to the SCO's Humvee for the mission briefing.

The Mission and the Map

The mission was time-sensitive; a helicopter was scheduled to pick us up within the hour. Our goal was to conduct an aerial route reconnaissance to assess the terrain's maneuverability and trafficability. We needed to ensure our Bradleys could successfully transit from the Port of Dammam, up the Tapline Road, and into our designated forward operating area without bogging down or getting caught in a bottleneck.

In those early days of the conflict, accurate maps were a rare and precious commodity. LTC Tucker asked that Captain Hicks provide one for the reconnaissance. He reached into his gear and produced his personal map, handing it to me with a look of stern, unyielding intensity.

"Do not give this map to anyone," he warned, his voice leaving no room for error. "I need it back."

"I understand, Sir," I assured him, tucking the paper away as if it were a holy relic. With the map secure, I stepped away to prepare for the flight. I spent those last moments in quiet conversation with the Lord, praying for the safety of my team and everyone involved in the mission. We were headed into the unknown, but I felt a strange, steady peace as we waited for the rhythmic thump of the Blackhawk's rotors.

Over the Berm and Under Fire

After meeting the helicopter crew in the heavy darkness before sunrise, I briefed the pilots on the specifics of our mission and coordinated the most effective route. We were soon airborne, the rotors cutting through the cool desert air as we flew toward the unknown. Within a brief time, we found ourselves within spitting distance of the Iraqi border.

The pilots were anxious, driven by a tense curiosity to get us as close to the line as possible so we could see exactly what we were up against. As we arrived at the border, the grim realities of the Republican Guard began to set in.

Looking down from the chopper, we saw the "suicide tanks"—T-72s positioned in dug-in emplacements with their tracks deliberately stripped away. It was a chilling testament to a command structure that did not trust its own men to stand their ground; these soldiers were forced to fight to the death because they had no means of retreat.

The atmosphere in the cabin shifted instantly from clinical observation to raw survival the moment the pilots yanked up the lead shields next to their seats. Suddenly, the sky was alive with tracers. They looked like glowing fireflies—beautiful in their luminescence but lethal in their intent—arching toward us as Iraqi soldiers opened fire.

Realizing the helicopter's floor offered little protection against rounds from below, I ordered my scouts to sit on their flak vests. We watched the tracers zip past our frame, praying silently as the pilots banked hard, pulling the chopper into a violent turn. They veered away from the border, pushing the engines toward the relative safety of the Saudi interior as we scrambled to find Tapline Road.

As we headed south toward the Port of Dammam, deeper into Saudi Arabia, we spotted a cluster of soldiers waving frantically near a traffic accident on Tapline Road. A military truck and a civilian vehicle had collided with devastating force. When the pilot asked if we should "Charlie Mike" (Continue the Mission) or land, my training took over. Back at Fort Sill, the Army had sent me to Emergency Medical Technician (EMT) school—a necessity for scouts who often work far beyond the reach of a dedicated medic. I told the pilot to land so we could evaluate the situation and decide whether I could offer any medical help.

We touched down, and I ran toward the twisted metal. The scene was grim; two civilians were clearly deceased. The soldiers involved had escaped with minor injuries, but their communications were dead. I had our pilots call in the recovery coordinates, and, with heavy hearts, we lifted off again to finish our route recon.

The Mission and the Brass

Upon our arrival at the Port of Dammam, we finally found our Squadron rear element. The scene was a chaotic sea of activity, housed in a massive hangar that served as the Squadron's assembly area. At once, I was intercepted by the Squadron Executive Officer (SXO), a Major who wasted no time pulling me aside for a report. I debriefed him on the route we had taken and pointed out specific areas on the map that I believed would be problematic for a convoy of our heavy vehicles. He was hospitable at first, offering us food and cots to rest our weary bones, but then came "the hook."

"Sergeant," he said, his tone shifting to one of command, "I do not have a map... I need to take yours."

My stomach dropped. Captain Hicks had been explicit and unwavering in his orders: *Bring that map back.* I knew the weight of my word, so I looked the Major in the eye and stood my ground as best a Sergeant could. "Sir, I told Captain Hicks I would bring his map back. I should keep my word."

It was a bold move, even a dangerous one, to challenge a Major. But he simply pulled rank, brushing off my concern with the cold logic of the chain of command. "I outrank him. If he gets upset, have him see me." With those words, the map—and my promise to Captain Hicks —disappeared into the SXO's hands. It was a situation well above my pay grade, and all I could do was stand there, empty-handed, and hope for the best.

Exhausted from the raw adrenaline of January 17th, Nielsen, Walker, and I finally collapsed onto our cots, desperate for sleep. We had barely drifted off when the silence was shattered by the piercing wail of sirens. Saddam Hussein had begun launching SCUD missiles at the port, and the hangar erupted into a panicked frenzy. Soldiers were scrambling in every direction, rushing to their assigned positions to set up a defensive perimeter "just in case" of a ground follow-up or a direct hit.

We, however, were just "temporary guests." We were three scouts with no assigned role in the port's defense, and our bodies had reached their absolute physical limit. We understood Saddam had used chemical weapons on the Kurds, and we did not intend to take any chances with a potential nerve agent. Without a word, we simply pulled on our protective masks, tightened the straps until they were airtight, and lay back down. In the middle of the shouting and the chaos, we went back to sleep. We had decided that if the end was coming, we would meet it resting.

The next morning, we met our flight crew and headed back to the forward assembly area in the northern desert. When we landed, I tracked down Captain Hicks and our Troop Executive Officer, Matt Weingast, who were huddled in a meeting over the hood of a

Humvee. I did not even have to open my mouth to explain the missing map. Hicks looked me up and down, read the situation instantly, and asked, "Did the good Major take my map?"

"Yes, sir," I replied, feeling a weight lift off my shoulders. "He pulled rank."

To my immense relief, he did not blow up. He just shook his head in that way officers do when dealing with the bureaucracy of higher command and said, "Okay, good job. You three get some chow."

A Final Watch

In the quiet, shimmering lulls of the desert, where the world's noise gave way to the low hum of the Bradley and the vast emptiness of the sand, Walker and I continued to grow closer. Walker was the kind of soldier who wore his heart on his sleeve once you got to know him. In the soft light of the evening, he showed me a picture of his girlfriend back home and spoke fondly of his family and his upbringing in Georgia. But as we sat there, away from the prying eyes of the rest of the unit, he revealed the heavy burden he carried beneath his professional exterior: his father had died, and he was consumed by a deep, burning anger at God for taking him.

I sat there in the silence, and my mind flashed back to my friend in California—the one who had died shortly after we had spoken about faith. I felt a sudden, pressing urge to do a better job for Walker than I had for my friend back then. I could not let another man I was responsible for walk into the unknown with a heart full of bitterness.

That night, we spent hours talking about God, our voices low against the desert wind. I tried to explain to him what I was taught, that God does not kill people; that is the enemy's work—to steal, kill, and destroy. I told him that God turns the things the enemy meant for evil into good. I was still learning myself, a "Scout" trying to navigate spiritual terrain I had not fully mapped out, and I remember straining to recall specific Scriptures to answer the hard, pointed questions he threw at me.

Eventually, I watched as the tension left his shoulders and he began to soften. Through our conversation, he realized his bitterness was not truly directed at God; he was simply a son who was hurting and mad at the hole his father's absence had left in his life. I watched that night as the Lord closed the distance between Himself and a grieving soldier. We were standing in a gap that had nothing to do with military tactics and everything to do with the soul.

SP Time Now

On February 1, 1991, the rhythm of our deployment shifted into a higher gear. Walker was tasked with leading a reconnaissance mission alongside several units from the squadron, which required precise coordination. While he prepared, I was ordered to stay back and oversee the ammunition breakdown in anticipation of the Bradley Fighting Vehicles' arrival—a tedious but critical job that ensured every belt and round was ready for distribution upon arrival.

Walker took the Humvee to refuel, weaving through the dust and diesel fumes to ensure the vehicle was topped off and combat-ready for the mission ahead. I remember the weight of that moment vividly; the desert has a way of swallowing time, and I knew we did not have a second to spare. Before he pulled away, I was clear with him, my voice cutting through the idling engines to emphasize the stakes. I told him directly that he needed to be back no later than 12:45pm. We had a hard SP (Start Point) time of 13:00 hours, and if we missed that one o'clock window, the entire synchronized movement of the squadron would be thrown into chaos.

I watched the Humvee disappear into the haze, the digital digits on my watch already feeling like a countdown.

By 12:50 pm, I was nervous. In the Cavalry, you *never* miss your SP time, and as his Sergeant, I felt responsible for his absence. But at 12:55 pm, with only five minutes to spare, he came rolling up in the Humvee.

Walker was a Non-Commissioned Officer's dream. He was never late, his uniform was always crisp, his boots were constantly shined, and his haircut was always strictly within regulations. We called new soldiers "Bean" because they are so green. Walker was different, like he always knew what he was doing, so we started calling him "Sprout." Still new, but not as green as others.

As he jumped out, I walked up and barked, "WHERE WERE YOU? You are cutting it awfully close! "He did not get defensive. He just looked at me and said, "I'm sorry, Sergeant. The water jugs were low, so I went to the water point and refilled them all."

I looked over at the patrol, everyone staged and ready to roll, with many vehicles from different troops, and the realization hit me: if Walker had not taken that initiative, they would not have had enough water for the mission. It was not even his responsibility—he was just using someone else's Humvee—but as Walker always did, he thought of his brothers before himself. I softened my tone. "Good job, Sprout," I said. "You did well... close, but good."

He gave me a laugh, settled into the vehicle, and they drove off on the mission. That was the last time I saw him alive. He was killed while on that patrol.

Numbness

I did not have the luxury of time to grieve. In the high-stakes vacuum of the desert, where every second demanded focus and every decision carried the weight of life or death, the process of mourning was an indulgence I simply could not afford. The hurt, the searing pain, the hollow sorrow, and the suffocating guilt—all of it had to be deferred.

There was no room for the luxury of processing these wounds while the mission remained unfinished.

Instead, I was forced to perform a brutal kind of mental triage. I had to shove every raw, bleeding emotion down into a dark, locked corner of my mind, bricking them up behind a wall of cold professionalism. I told myself I was merely saving them for later, storing them away for a future time when survival was no longer the immediate, crushing priority. I knew the bill would eventually come due, but for now, the only way to lead and endure was to remain hollowed out and hyper-focused on the task at hand.

Putting a Life in a Box

I moved through the time that followed like a ghost, floating through the hollow process of packing up his personal gear and belongings. There is a specific, painful cruelty in the act of folding a man's life into a box—sorting through the mundane and the intimate, the dirty laundry, and the letters from home, until a human existence is reduced to a shipping weight. I was completely numb, a passenger in my own body, simply going through the motions as I learned the brutal art of disengaging my feelings. I had to become a machine; if I let the reality of what I was holding break through the surface, I knew I would not be able to finish the task.

The squadron held a memorial service, a stark and somber gathering of dust-covered soldiers, in the middle of a world that refused to stop turning. I stood before the unit and spoke about Walker—about the man he was and the void he left behind—and then stood in the heavy, suffocating silence to listen to the soul-piercing notes of *Taps*. To this day, the memory of that speech is a total blank. I cannot remember a single word I said. The man who stood at that podium was a version of me I no longer recognize—someone who had successfully pushed his soul into a dark corner just to survive the sound of that bugle.

Charlie Mike

I knew I had to push through and continue the mission. Soon, the horizon began to rumble, but this time it was not with the distant thud of falling bombs. It was the familiar, guttural growl of heavy engines. Our Bradley Fighting Vehicles—our iron lifelines—finally rolled into the assembly area, kicking up plumes of dust as they arrived.

We reclaimed them by platoon, moving with a practiced urgency to set up a 360-degree defensive perimeter. Immediately, we set to work stretching out the "camo" netting, breaking up the vehicles' hard silhouettes to hide them from aerial observation.

After weeks of living exposed in the sand, having our "home away from home" back changed the entire energy of the troop. There is a specific kind of comfort a scout feels inside the cramped, oily hull of a Bradley; it is a fortress and a sanctuary all at once, permeated by the smell of diesel.

We set to the task of preparing for war with a renewed, lethal focus. We zeroed the 25mm chain guns, ensuring our primary weapon was precise. We slid the heavy TOW missiles into their launchers and packed the floorboards with crates of C4 and TNT, preparing for any obstacle the Iraqis might throw in our path.

We were no longer just observers watching from afar. The "Spearhead" was sharp, anxious, and primed. We were ready for the storm we knew was coming, and we were determined to be the ones who broke it.

The Deluge Before the Storm

Just as we were making our final preparations for the ground war, I was tapped for duty. Our Bradleys were positioned in a tactical "laager"—a 360-degree circle for mutual protection. Despite the heavy armor, we had to keep armed foot patrols around the entire squadron's perimeter. This needed a Sergeant of the Guard to oversee the rotation and ensure every sector remained secure. I was the lucky Non-Commissioned Officer (NCO) whose name came up next on the roster.

It was a grueling 24-hour shift that began at 6:00 am. The day started out deceptively calm, though the sky eventually turned a heavy, bruised gray. Then, the unthinkable happened in a land known for its aridity: it started to rain.

Saudi Arabia typically receives only about 3.5 inches of rain in an entire year, but that night, the sky broke open and gave us the annual total all at once. The temperature plummeted. It was not just a drizzle; it was a torrential downpour driven by a relentless, biting wind. I was not prepared for the cold, and as the hours ticked by, I became soaked to the bone and frozen through. By the time I was finally relieved at 6:00 am the next morning, I was in a bad way.

Shaking with fever and chills, I made my way to the medics' Armored Personnel Carrier (APC). The "Doc" looked me over and delivered a grim diagnosis: "Good news is it is walking pneumonia," he said. "Bad news is, all I can give you is aspirin." I felt as if I had been run over and dragged for miles, but there was no time for a hospital bed. I had to get back to my vehicle and continue preparing for the looming battle.

Beyond the Berm: The Second Recon

Within days, the orders we had been waiting for finally came down. Up until this point, we had been a safe distance from the Iraqi border, but under the cover of darkness, we moved the entire unit closer to the berm, still just out of range.

Despite my fever and the weight of the pneumonia, I was tasked with my second reconnaissance mission of the war. This time, I took five other scouts with me: Joe Farmer, Nielsen, Dave Baker, Monty

Tolleson, and Hans Gukeisen. Our mission was to conduct a forward recon patrol up to and around the massive sand berm, scanning for any signs of enemy movement or life beyond the disabled "suicide" tanks we had seen from the air.

The desert at night, through Night Vision Devices (NVDs), is a world of grainy green shadows where depth perception is a constant struggle. We did not encounter any living enemy soldiers, but the tension was so high that we were seeing ghosts in the shadows. At one point, Nielsen and Baker spotted a dark shape that was difficult to identify through the NVDs. Thinking it was an enemy combatant, they executed a textbook combat assault—only to discover they had successfully neutralized a desert bush.

We returned to our lines with the intel the commander needed, my lungs burning and my body exhausted, but ready. We were now at the doorstep of Iraq, and the ground war was only hours away.

The Reality of Faith

The silence of the desert was heavy, broken only by the low, mechanical hum of the Bradley Fighting Vehicle's engine and the constant, static-filled crackle of the radio. It was in these moments of isolation that Psalm 23 stopped being a memorized poem and became a reality: "Even though I walk through the valley of the shadow of death, I will fear no evil, for you are with me..." As a scout, you live in that shadow. You are always out front, exposed, and vulnerable, waiting for the first shot to ring out. But as I sat in the darkness of the BFV, I realized that the "shadow" of death is not death itself; a shadow is simply proof that a Light is shining nearby, casting that shadow.

12

THE END AROUND

In 1991, the movement known as the "End Around"—often hailed as the "Thunder Run"—entered military history. The Third Armored Division surged forward with staggering, unrelenting speed, navigating a landscape that looked more like the end of the world than a battlefield. Retreating forces had ignited the oil wells, creating massive, roiling pillars of fire that choked the sky with soot. The smoke was so dense it swallowed the sun, turning high noon into a pitch-black midnight.

We lived and fought under the constant, suffocating threat of chemical weapons, our nerves stretched thin by the persistent howl of gas alarms. While the aluminum and steel armor of our Bradleys served as our primary physical defense against shrapnel and heat, I found myself relying heavily on a different kind of protection—the spiritual armor I had studied in Ephesians 6 during my youth.

No Atheists in Foxholes

There is a timeless adage born of combat: *there are no atheists in foxholes.* I saw the truth of this firsthand as the veneer of bravado stripped away under fire. Soldiers who had previously professed a total lack of belief, or who had never uttered a prayer in their lives, began approaching me in the quiet, tense lulls between movements. They asked me how to speak to God and sought the comfort of prayer. Over the course of the war, I shared as much as I knew, kneeling in the sand or leaning against cold steel to pray with them.

To me, the "Shield of Faith" was never a mere metaphor or a poetic Sunday school lesson; it was a tangible spiritual barrier that quenched the fiery darts of paralyzing fear. There were countless moments where we were closer to death than we could have realized —moments where the line between survival and catastrophe was razor-thin—and yet, we were shielded. In the heat of the "Thunder Run," I stood firmly on the promise of 2 Samuel 22:3, which declares: *"He is my shield, the power that saves me, and my place of safety."*

As a scout screening for the division, the "protector" I had resolved to become back in Lawton was finally standing his post. We found ourselves at the tip of the spear in the largest tank battle since WWII —the Battle of 73 Easting and Phase Line Bullet. These engagements were part of a massive "left hook" maneuver designed to encircle and destroy the Iraqi Republican Guard. As we crossed the desert at high speed, visibility was often zero, choked by blinding sandstorms and the thick, black, oily smoke belching from sabotaged wells.

To keep our spirits up as we surged into the heart of Iraq, I would read Scripture over the Bradleys' internal communication system. Amidst the static of the radio and the roar of the engine, I wanted to build my crew's faith from the inside out.

As we sped across the desert, the sky was split in two. On one side, there was a clear, peaceful blue; on the other, a deep, dark purple and black mass that was moving toward us. In that moment, I knew it was not just a weather front—it was a manifestation of good and evil. I could feel in my spirit the physical, mental, and spiritual warfare that lay just ahead. The atmosphere was charged with a heavy, supernatural weight. As soon as the darkness of that storm covered us, the radio cracked loudly with the chilling words, *"Contact East,"* as our lead units slammed into the enemy line.

The Battle of 73 Easting and Phase Line Bullet

The Battle of 73 Easting was a violent, high-speed meeting engagement. We were moving across a featureless desert where "73 Easting" was simply a north-south coordinate on a map. Our Bradley Fighting Vehicles and M1A1 Abrams tanks slammed into the Iraqi defense lines, using thermal sights to engage the enemy through the dust and darkness. We were significantly outnumbered, but our training and technology provided a lethal edge.

Phase Line Bullet was a critical boundary where the 3rd Armored Division—my division—met the elite Tawakalna Division of the Republican Guard. Our unit was the first in the 3rd Armored to engage this heavily armored force. The "Bullet" line became a wall of fire. It was here that some of the most intense, close-quarters armored combat took place. We fought through a labyrinth of bunkers and dug-in T-72 tanks, fulfilling our mission as the screen protecting the division's main body.

Our unit was engaged every single day of that 100-hour ground war. We moved with a relentless momentum, and we were among the first to enter "Free Kuwait," seeing the liberation of a people who had been under the heel of an occupier.

The Cost of the Mission

But the victory came with a heavy, hollow price. We lost amazing soldiers in Iraq—men of character who gave everything they had for the person standing to their left and right. Edwin Kutz, Kenneth Gentry, and Charles Scott Walker... they are the true heroes of this story. Their names are etched not just in stone, but in the hearts of those of us who made it back.

The tragedy did not end when the 100 hours were up. Hans Gukeisen, a brother-in-arms, went on to pursue his dream after Desert Storm, attending school to become an Army helicopter pilot. He returned to Iraq during the later conflict, still wanting to serve. While flying a mission to Medivac an injured child—an act of pure mercy—his Blackhawk helicopter struck a power line and plunged into the Euphrates River, killing everyone onboard.

These men lived out the ultimate sacrifice described in John 15:13: "Greater love has no one than this, than to lay down one's life for his friends." I carry their memory with me into every ministry and every battle I face today. They were the ones who stood in the gap when it mattered most.

I suffered deeply because of Charles Scott Walker's death. As his leader, I felt a crushing weight of responsibility for him, and the fact that I could not be right beside him when he was killed tore at me. In the aftermath, I went through the "shoulda, coulda, woulda" cycle a million times in my head—a relentless mental loop that offered no exit. I struggled with vivid nightmares and spent countless nights unable to sleep, paralyzed by a mixture of survivor's guilt and remorse.

Not only was Walker my soldier, but I genuinely liked him. He had a spark in him; I knew without a doubt that he would succeed in whatever he touched in life. In the silence of those sleepless nights, I found myself wondering about our conversations. I replayed our talks about God repeatedly, desperately hoping the seeds we planted had taken root and wondering if he had truly made his peace with the Lord before the end.

Despite the pain of those losses, I am truly thankful to have served alongside some of the best men ever to wear the uniform. These were men of grit and integrity who stood firm when the world was on fire. Names like Terry Tucker, Ronald Sneed, Jeff Hicks, Matt Weingast, Ed Languinski, Willie Choice, Randy Pee, Steve Reynolds, Vinson Sexton, Eric Sanders, and Stanley Davis, along with the others I have mentioned previously, are etched into my memory.

Although there are too many others to name individually, every one of them will always hold a special, sacred place in my heart. We were forged in the same furnace, and the bond we shared is something the passage of time can never erode. They were not just a unit; they were a brotherhood.

These men sharpened me. They prepared me for the battles I would face long after I took off the uniform. Even the guilt I carried for Walker eventually had to be surrendered to the same Foundation I shared with my crew—the realization that while I was a protector, there is only One true Savior.

The Scout Comes Home

I returned from the war a changed man, though I did not yet realize the full extent of the transformation. I spent a few more years stationed in Germany, primarily focusing on finishing my bachelor's degree. My roadmap for the future was set. I planned to attend school to become a Physician's Assistant. I was heading steadily in that direction when the Army intervened, and I received orders for Drill Sergeant School at Fort Jackson, South Carolina.

Beneath the surface of my academic pursuits and daily duties, a silent battle was raging. I was struggling with the loss of my friends, and I had not yet faced the deep-seated pain and hurt building up inside me. That unresolved trauma slowly started to manifest itself through recurring nightmares and a persistent lack of sleep. I was a "Scout" who was finally running out of horizon; I needed to slow down and quit running from the pain.

During this season, Lieutenant Brian Sperling and his wife, Joanna, were dear friends of ours—the kind of friends who become like family through the shared trials of military life. During the intensity of Operations Desert Shield and Desert Storm, Brian had served as one of our Cobra attack helicopter pilots. He was the guardian in the sky, providing the lethal air support that we relied on so heavily from the ground.

After we returned from the desert, Brian took over the Area Support Team (AST) in Büdingen, Germany. This was a vital role, as the AST served as the connective tissue between our local military base and the German community. He handled complex security matters and navigated the inevitable friction or issues that arose between the two cultures.

While I was in the transition period before leaving Germany, I accepted a position on Brian's Area Support Team. This role was a true blessing. It afforded me the flexibility to dedicate more time to my schooling while simultaneously navigating the mountain of paperwork needed to out-process and prepare for our move to Fort Jackson.

More importantly, it gave me the margin I desperately needed to reflect. For the first time, I began to deal with the losses I had suffered and the crushing weight of responsibility I felt for those who did not come home. While I did not deal with it as thoroughly as I could have —or should have—at the time, I did finally begin to scratch the surface. I knew then that there was much more work to be done in my soul before I could effectively lead and train the next generation of soldiers.

13

BACK TO THE STATES

Fort Jackson, South Carolina, was vastly different from any post I had ever been stationed at. As a combat arms soldier, I was conditioned to the "high-speed, low-drag" environment of the frontline units—a world where you were given a clear mission, and the command structure provided the unwavering support needed to execute it.

In that world, results were the only currency that mattered. However, during my time at Ft. Jackson, I discovered a stark reality that departed from the cavalry life I knew. Based on my experience, the culture shifted toward a facade; it became more about how things "looked" on the surface than how they "were" in reality.

The transition was incredibly difficult for me. There was a palpable shift in the Army's mindset under a new administration, one that seemed to erode the discipline the service so desperately needed. To me, that discipline is not just about following rules for the sake of it; it is the absolute requirement for survival in life-and-death combat situations.

Watching those standards soften was a hard pill to swallow for someone who had seen exactly what happens when things go wrong in the heat of battle. I found myself navigating a system that prioritized optics over the raw, hardcore readiness that keeps soldiers alive.

The Last Straw

One morning, I was correcting a female soldier for not wearing her dog tags inside her uniform—again. As I spoke, I twirled the chain that held the metal tags around my finger, holding them up before her face as a visual aid to my point. "Where are these supposed to be, Private?" I asked. She replied in a dull, monotone voice, "In my uniform, Drill Sergeant," and went through the slow-motion performance of tucking them away.

I had dealt with her several times before; her bunk was never made correctly, and her uniform was consistently substandard. She obviously did not want to be there. After my experience in the desert, I was hyper-focused on ensuring all trainees paid close attention to detail—because I knew firsthand that, in combat, it's the details that keep you alive.

Later that day, the atmosphere shifted. I received word to gather my chain of command and report to the Brigade Commander's office at once. After I informed my leadership, we were all ushered into the office, where the Commander—a Colonel—sat alongside a Captain who identified himself as the Brigade Chaplain. I reported to the Commander at attention and continued to receive the most intense butt-chewing I have had since basic training.

Once he finished with me, he turned his fury toward my Battalion Commander, who had gone with me. It turned out that the young female recruit I had corrected earlier had gone straight to the Chaplain. She claimed that I had choked her with her dog tags and that she was now both emotionally and physically injured.

I saw red. I stood there at rigid attention, forced to remain silent while being denied the opportunity to tell my version of the lie. When the Colonel was finished, my Battalion Commander chimed in, declaring that he was not going to allow a "subpar NCO" to diminish or tarnish the Brigade's perfect record of zero trainee abuse.

The words "subpar NCO" stung like a physical blow. I was a combat-tested soldier with an outstanding record. I had no blemishes, no reprimands, and no marks anywhere in my files. My career trajectory had been a vertical climb: I had gone from Private E-1 to Staff Sergeant E-6 in just four and a half years, and I had just made the E-7 (Sergeant First Class) list at seven and a half years. I was 25 years old and moving right along, a high performer by every Army metric.

To be treated in this manner—to have my character assassinated based on a fabrication after everything I had given to the service—was the final straw. The "protector" who had screened for the 3rd Armored Division was being betrayed by the very institution he was trying to strengthen.

The administration at the time was pushing heavily for a "kinder, gentler" military. In my opinion, this cultural shift was not just a change in tone—it was actively weakening our nation's defense. We were transitioning away from the hard-nosed, combat-ready standards that had seen us through the desert and moving toward a system that prioritized optics and sensitivity over readiness and discipline.

Moving On

The "broken protector" in me saw this clearly. In a world where the Wichita Mountains still stood as a testament to harsh realities and the sands of Iraq had recently shown us the lethality of the Republican Guard, this softening felt like a betrayal of the mission. We were not training people for a corporate office; we were training them to survive and win in the most unforgiving environments on

Earth. By lowering the bar and entertaining every complaint without due process—like the false accusation I was currently facing—the leadership was eroding the very backbone of the NCO corps.

The focus had shifted from preparing soldiers for the harshness of the "dead space" to protecting the "perfect record" of a brigade. It was a symptom of a larger problem: when you start to value the institution's reputation more than the truth and the integrity of the men standing in the gap, the foundation begins to crumble. This realization, combined with how I was being treated, made it clear that the path I was on was no longer aligned with the values that had shaped me before the world ever touched me. I felt the unmistakable shift of a new chapter beginning. Life was changing rapidly; with the birth of our second son, my wife and I shared a deep, quiet realization that it was time to take the next significant step in our journey.

I had spent years serving my country on the global stage, facing the grit of the Mojave and the fires of the Persian Gulf. Now, however, I felt a new calling stirring within me—a desire to take the discipline and strength I had forged in the Army and use it to serve my community closer to home. The warrior was preparing to become a neighbor, and the path forward was finally becoming clear. I began my exit from the military, packing up and moving the family back home.

I headed back to Oklahoma and was accepted into the police academy. The transition felt natural; the scout was coming home, ready to resume the role of protector on the streets of the place that raised him. The uniform had changed, but the mission stayed the same.

14

THE THIN BLUE LINE

Returning to Lawton, Oklahoma, was like stepping back into a story I had left unfinished. The red dirt was the same—that iron-rich, stubborn clay that stains your shoes and stays in the creases of your skin like a permanent mark of origin. The wind still carried that familiar Oklahoma weight, a relentless pressure that pushes against you as if trying to test your resolve, and the Wichita Mountains still stood watch over the horizon like silent, granite elders, unchanged by the passage of time.

But I was not the same kid who had huddled in a storm shelter as a tornado roared overhead, nor was I the same gullible boy who had stood still for his brother's "bravery test." I was a man who had seen the "green sky" of Iraq through night-vision goggles and the white-hot, twisted metal of desert vehicle crashes. I had been forged and refined in the furnace of the Army, but Lawton was calling me back to a different kind of frontline. I eventually traded my Army greens for the blue of the Police Department.

Joining the police department was not just a career choice or a way to earn a paycheck; it was a direct continuation of my calling to stand in the gap between the vulnerable and the predator. I transitioned from a Bradley Fighting Vehicle to a patrol car, and from the shifting, treacherous sands of the Middle East to the cracked asphalt streets of my own hometown.

It was a transition that felt both jarring and deeply right—a full-circle moment in the narrative of my life. I was back in the very neighborhoods where I had once walked miles to church with my mom, our Sunday shoes clicking on the pavement. I found myself patrolling the same streets where Darlene and Phil had once dropped off that Thanksgiving miracle, proving once again that grace can be delivered in a heavy aluminum tray.

As a police officer, I was no longer just seeing the landscape; I handled it. I was a "Scout" for my community, navigating the local "dead spaces" and identifying threats before they could strike, and I took that mantle seriously. I was back on the ground that raised me, armed with the discipline of a soldier and the heart of a protector, ready to serve the people who shared my roots.

The Ghosts of Lawton

Lawton, however, had its own shadows. It is a town where the light of the plains can be blindingly bright, but the dark corners are deep. I soon found myself working in a world that needed a different kind of vigilance than the military. In the Army, typically, the enemy often had a uniform, a flag, and a somewhat clear frontline. You knew where the "wire" was. In law enforcement, the enemy was often a ghost—a cycle of addiction, trauma, and desperation that reminded me all too much of the "shadows" my father had struggled with throughout my childhood.

Every time I met someone lost in a bottle or staring with the hollow eyes of a needle-user, I did not see a criminal to be processed; I saw the "why" that had haunted my father. I saw the ghost of my brother Ronnie bleeding out in 1957, and the way that pain had driven a man to drown his soul in alcohol. I saw the pain of men and women who were trying to make the world stop hurting by any means necessary.

It was here, on the streets of my hometown, that my faith and my duty merged into one. I realized that God had not just strategically placed people in my life to save me from car wrecks and tornadoes— He had strategically placed me back in Lawton to be a shield for others. I was a Lawton kid, an Army Scout, and now a police officer, but I was a man doing his part. I stepped onto the force with the same mindset I had in the 4th Squadron, 7th Cavalry: eyes open, ears tuned, moving toward the trouble so others would not have to.

I realized that the job included the dark, trash-strewn alleys of Lawton and the tense, screaming domestic calls at 3:00 am when the air is thick with the smell of spilled beer and regret. God was not just in the desert of Iraq or the hills of Fort Knox; He rode in the passenger seat of my patrol car.

Learning the Ropes

Learning to be a police officer on the streets of Lawton, Oklahoma, was a ride like no other. You honestly think you know the town you grew up in, but I soon realized you only know what you were exposed to as a child. Every city and town in the world has two faces: the side they want everyone to see and the side they want no one to know about. I spent most of my time in law enforcement trying to keep that hidden side out of the headlines. More times than I can count, I saw events being covered up or obscured to prevent the city from knowing exactly what happened, where it occurred, or who was involved. As much as you do not want to expect it or believe it, politics plays a massive role in how policing is executed in our country.

I worked long, grueling hours training for the job and then keeping the rule of law during my shifts. I patrolled the very same streets we played on as kids, and I remembered fondly how we used to walk up to police cars in our neighborhood to get football trading cards. Back then, we always said "Yes, sir" or "No, sir," and we felt safe whenever we saw those old red-and-white cars with the lights on top.

However, it was a completely different story when I finally hit the street myself, anxious and ready to keep the city safe. I will never forget the first group of kids I drove by in my old neighborhood. I had prepared beforehand by buying a stack of trading cards from the store, hoping to recreate the magic I remembered. As I pulled up, the oldest of a group of five young teenagers, ranging from twelve to fifteen years old, sneered, "What the f*** do you want, cracker?"

I was stunned. All of them laughed as he put on his show of bravado. When I asked where they lived, he snapped back, "None of your business, a**hole." I am sure I looked visibly confused as my training officer pulled up and spent about ten minutes dealing with the group. After they left, he looked at me and said, "Not like it used to be, is it?" He started laughing and reminded me that we need to ensure we "update our weapons" for the times—meaning our communication styles and tactics for dealing with people from all levels of society. I had assumed I would have an inside edge because I was raised in the area, but I was wrong.

The Welfare Check

As my training progressed, I spent more time in the area and slowly became acclimated to the rhythm of the neighborhoods. Over time, I developed close, genuine contacts—salt-of-the-earth people who just wanted to live their lives in safety and security. They were the kind of people who would reach out in times of trouble and, touchingly, even remembered my birthday. I took my responsibility to them personally, doing my best to ensure my patrol zone remained a safe place for them.

I had many elderly residents in my zone and made it a habit to check on them whenever the shift allowed. However, working from the late afternoon into the early morning hours made this difficult, as most of my older residents turned in early.

One evening, dispatch radioed me to perform a welfare check on a senior citizen whom neighbors had not seen in several days. I arrived at the address and was met by another officer to conduct a courtesy walkthrough. As we approached the front door, the tell-tale signs of a problem were at once clear: the mailbox was overflowing, spilling mail onto the porch, and a pile of uncollected newspapers lay scattered around the entrance.

Forced Entry

We knocked persistently for several minutes, with no response, before circling the house and peeking into windows for any sign of movement. A neighbor soon approached, a phone pressed to her ear. She told us the homeowner was a woman who was usually outside every day but had disappeared. The neighbor explained she was currently on the line with the woman's daughter, who wanted to speak with us.

I took the phone, and the daughter explained that while she owned the home, she was currently away on business. She had moved her mother in to care for her as she aged. Sensing the gravity of the situation, she gave us clear permission to force entry if necessary. We radioed in the update and tried to breach the doors, but both the front and back entrances were reinforced with double deadbolts. They were far more stubborn than we had expected.

The Bathroom Window

Searching for a weaker point of entry, we noticed a small window about seven feet off the ground that was cracked open. Based on its height and size, we assumed it was a bathroom window. I had the other officer boost me up so I could reach the frame and shove it high enough to squeeze through. Once it was open as far as it would go, my partner gave me another heave. I grabbed the sill, pulling with everything I had to hoist my head and shoulders through the narrow gap.

Since the sun had already set, the interior was a void of pitch-black shadows. I was precariously balanced in the frame, unable to reach for my flashlight without losing my grip. As I tried to ease forward blindly, unsure of the drop distance to the floor, my hands slipped. I tumbled headfirst into the room.

I crashed into what I later discovered was a laundry basket brimming with towels and clothes, which fortunately dampened my fall. I sat there for a moment in the dark, chuckling to myself at the absurdity of the landing as I fumbled for the flashlight on my belt. But as I reached for the light, an uncanny, prickling feeling washed over me— the distinct sensation that I was not alone.

When the beam of my flashlight finally cut through the heavy dark, I realized my instinct had been chillingly correct. The elderly woman was right there, unmistakably deceased, leaning against the wall merely inches from where I had landed. The sight was so sudden and so jarring in the silence of that pitch-black room that, before I could even process what I was looking at, the loudest, shrillest scream I had ever heard in my life pierced the stillness of the house. It took several agonizing seconds of echoing vibration for me to realize that the sound was coming from my own throat.

Once the initial shock subsided and the scene was secured, the gravity of the moment was quickly replaced by the relentless ribbing that comes with police work. Thanks to my fellow officer—who wasted no time sharing the story of my "operatic" discovery—I became the reluctant star of the shift. From that night on, every time a welfare check came across the radio, the airwaves would crackle with my colleagues' voices. They would call me up, mock pleading for me to handle the call just so they could see if I could hit a higher note or scream even louder this time. It was the kind of hazing that only happens among people who deal with the grim reality of death every day; my moment of pure, unadulterated terror had become the shift's favorite new legend.

The job was full of laughs and ribbing, but it also brought moments of pure devastation.

Heartbreak

I will never forget a house fire in one of the poorest neighborhoods in the city, where a family of five was killed in their trailer. The Christmas cards they had pinned up around their door had drifted too close to a heater and ignited in the middle of the night. I arrived with other officers just as the back end of the trailer was fully engulfed. We ran inside and began pulling children out through the smoke. When we could no longer stand the heat, we moved to the grass and started administering CPR.

I was performing compressions and breathing for a little girl no older than six when the paramedics arrived and took over. I knew that she was gone, and once again, I felt numb from loss, and that familiar, heavy feeling of helplessness started to spread over me. It was only when I went back to the station to start the paperwork that I noticed the radio microphone clipped to my shoulder epaulet. It was melted. The fire had been so intense that the rubber casing had liquefied and run down the mic's face.

On that night, I cried out in my spirit for that family. My melted microphone was a physical reminder of the heat of the battle, but the weight on my heart was a reminder that being a "protector" often means standing in the gap between life and death, even when the outcome breaks your heart.

Nick of Time

Soon after, I found out firsthand that sometimes your timeliness—and your willingness to listen to a still, small voice—makes the ultimate difference between life and death.

One night, Lawton was being hammered by a violent electrical storm. The lightning arced across the sky in a way only an Oklahoma storm can, and the rain was a continuous, driving sheet of water, making visibility zero. No one wanted to be out in it, but I received a call to conduct a "welfare check." A man's brother was worried because he had not been heard from in over a day. Normally, this might not seem urgent, but the brother insisted they had spoken every single morning for years, and he had never once missed a call.

It was about 9:00 pm, pitch black, and the rain was coming down harder than ever. I met another officer at the location, and we trudged to the trailer's door, getting instantly drenched. We knocked three or four times, but with no answer, we retreated to our patrol cars to get out of the deluge. We sat there for a minute as thunder boomed and lightning cracked the sky like a scene from a horror movie. I radioed my supervisor to ask if we should keep trying or return later. He suggested we wait about ten minutes until the weather dies down a bit.

I put the car in drive, but right as I was about to pull away, my spirit nudged me. That deep-seated, still-small voice was telling me to stop. I radioed dispatch and told them we were going to try one more time. As we both headed back to the door, a massive crack of thunder rocked the trailer, and all the lights in the neighborhood went out.

In the sudden darkness, we turned on our flashlights and knocked even louder. Still nothing. My discernment was causing my heart to race; I knew something was wrong. Legally, we could not force entry without a "plain view" or "plain hearing" of distress, but as I reached out to try the doorknob, I felt it "give." The door swung open into the trailer.

We stepped inside, calling out our presence. With the power out, the interior was a void, illuminated only by our flashlights and the strobing flashes of lightning through the windows. The other officer went right, and I headed left toward the kitchen, still calling out.

Police officers have a specific tactic for clearing dark rooms: we shine the beam of our high-intensity flashlights directly at the white ceiling. This diffuses the light, illuminating the entire room more evenly. Unfortunately, because my light was pointed up, I could not see the floor clearly. As I passed the kitchen, I suddenly slipped on the linoleum and fell hard on my side next to a small bathroom.

My flashlight hit the ground and rolled, its beam instantly cutting across a large pool of blood. In the center of the bathroom lay a man dressed only in his underwear, positioned in an even larger pool of blood. I felt like a cartoon character—my feet spinning in place as I tried to stand up and run backward at the same time, slipping again in the slick red mess.

I yelled for the other officer. He came running with his gun drawn as I regained my balance and retrieved my blood-stained flashlight. The man was pale as a ghost and had many small stab wounds to his chest and stomach. He had lost so much blood that the floor was completely covered, but the most unsettling part was seeing the wounds slowly "gape" open and closed.

I reached down and felt the faintest, smallest tap of a pulse. My partner called for an immediate medical response. We stayed by him, reassuring him that help was on the way and offering comfort until the ambulance arrived. The paramedics were grim; they confirmed his chances were slim at best. Standing there in that blacked-out trailer, covered in his blood, I said a prayer for him without delay.

After getting cleaned up, I headed to the hospital to finish the paperwork, my mind still replaying the strobing lightning and the slick linoleum. To my absolute shock, the doctor came out and told us he expected the man to live. They had pumped his depleted system full of blood and meticulously stitched up the gaping wounds, and despite the odds, he was recovering well. The doctor looked me square in the eye and said, "If he had spent ten minutes more on that floor, he would be dead." The weight of those ten minutes sat heavily on me. It was the exact amount of time my supervisor had suggested we wait, and the exact window of time that would have closed forever if I had not listened to that spiritual nudge.

The mystery of the "horror movie" scene was solved a brief time later. We found out from the detectives working the case that this was not a random act of violence or a home invasion gone wrong. It was a cold, calculated betrayal: his own wife had tried to kill him to collect on insurance money. She had left him there to bleed out in the dark, confident that the storm would hide her crime and that no one would find him until it was too late.

It was a chilling reminder of the "hidden side" of the city I had grown to know. While the storm raged outside, an even more violent storm had taken place inside that home. The darkness of that trailer could not hide the truth, and the wife's plan was thwarted by a mere 10 minutes and a prompt from the Holy Spirit.

Standing in the hospital hallway, I realized that being a protector meant more than just stopping speeders or catching thieves; it meant being an instrument of intervention in the moments when the enemy thinks he has already won.

If I had leaned on my own understanding or the supervisor's advice, I would have driven away. God used that "nudge" to perform a miracle, proving that a protector's greatest tool is not always his belt or his training—it is his discernment.

Never a dull moment

Patrol work was an endless stream of domestic disturbances, crimes against people, crimes against property, crimes against animals, traffic violations, warrants, and ultimately drugs. I had a knack for finding illicit drugs when dealing with people on routine patrol or on traffic calls.

One day, while on patrol, I spotted a vehicle without functioning brake lights. This is an obvious and immediate safety hazard, as there is no way for trailing drivers to see when the vehicle is slowing down or coming to a complete stop. I called the plate into dispatch, activated my emergency lights, and gave a quick blast of my air horn to signal the driver to pull over.

The driver complied, but as I shifted the squad car into park, he quickly jumped out of his vehicle and began walking toward me with a determined stride. I at once jumped out of my car, put my arm out for distance, and commanded, "Whoa, slow down! Stop right there." In law enforcement, it is never a good idea to let a subject approach you while you are still seated; you never want to be caught in a position where your mobility is restricted.

Instantly, before I could even explain the reason for the stop, the man rattled off, "I know you pulled me over because I have eight ounces of meth in my car, but it's not mine, and I'm taking it right back to its owner!"

As my mind raced to catch up with his unsolicited confession, I realized just how incredibly paranoid he was. He was acting "tweaked out," his eyes darting around as if he were convinced someone was watching his every move from the shadows. I kept my voice calm and told him it was okay, explaining that I would have him take a seat in my patrol car while I checked things out. He was so far gone that he asked if I wanted to put handcuffs on him, to which I replied, "Well, yes. Yes, I do."

He turned around and "assumed the position" without resistance while I secured the cuffs and patted him down for any weapons or items that might cause us harm. Once I had him safely in the back of my car, I asked him, "So, I can search your car for drugs?"

He did not hesitate: "Yes, but the ten ounces of meth aren't mine."

I noted the jump in quantity—now it was ten ounces. "Okay, thank you," I said, and continued to search the vehicle.

Sure enough, the search yielded far more than his paranoid estimates. Hidden in the car were 16 ounces (a full pound) of methamphetamines and two pounds of marijuana. It was a significant amount of poison to take off the streets, and it ended up being the easiest drug seizure I ever made.

Sometimes, a person's own guilt and paranoia do more to bring them to justice than any high-tech surveillance ever could. That driver was so desperate to explain away his "burden" that he walked himself right into a pair of handcuffs, proving that in the battle between the protector and the criminal, sometimes the truth just wants to be told.

15

THE BELLY OF THE BEAST

Moving into narcotics work was like stepping into the belly of the beast. My job was to go where most people avoid—the "trap houses," the backroom deals, and the places where lives are traded for a fix. This work required a different kind of vigilance. It required the "Scout" mindset, but also a reliance on a sense of discernment I did not even realize I had until I was tested in the fire.

Working undercover or during high-stakes drug busts, I was constantly reminded of Daniel in the lion's den. When he was thrown into the lions' den, it was not his rank or his status that saved him; it was his God. **Daniel 6:22** (NIV): "My God sent his angel, and he shut the mouths of the lions. They have not hurt me..." I was not walking the consistent walk of a Christian, but before each shift, I would pray for protection.

There were nights in narcotics where the "lions" were very real people with nothing to lose, their brains rewired by chemicals, with weapons within reach. Yet repeatedly, I felt a hedge of protection that defied logic. I saw the absolute devastation of sin—families torn apart, children neglected—but I also knew there were others called by God to stand in the gap that keeps a city from tearing itself apart. I learned that you cannot shine a light unless you are willing to walk into the dark.

During my years in uniform, the line between "Officer" and "Christian" began to blur. I was not just enforcing statutes; I was seeing the brokenness of the human condition in its rawest form. I started to see my badge as a symbol of authority, yes, but also as a platform for peace. I learned that a calm word spoken with the authority of Christ could do more than a pair of handcuffs ever could.

Discerning Discernment

I was learning that you can enforce the law with one hand while holding out a lifeline of hope with the other. I quickly found out I was adept at reading people. I had no idea at the time that it was the spiritual gift of discernment. To me, it just felt like a "gut feeling." To help refine this, I was sent to an Interview and Interrogation course. There, I learned about neural linguistics—how the eyes move when the brain accesses memory versus when it constructs a lie—and how to read the subtle body language of deception.

Soon, I was transferred to Special Operations to serve on a special assignment and work on narcotics, getting my feet wet. It was a world of masks and hidden identities.

I will never forget my partner and me pulling up to a light in our unmarked car. We were in plainclothes, looking like anything but police officers. Two ladies walked up to our window and asked if we wanted "company."

As I looked at them, I could "feel" them. I could sense the deep, stabbing pain they were in. An instant compassion arose in me, an almost overwhelming feeling. My partner, playing the role, said, " Sure, we could use some company." One of the ladies, cautious and streetwise, asked if we were police. He laughed and said, "No, are you?" They started laughing and hopped into the car without any hesitation.

As plainclothes officers, we had our police radios clipped to the car's visors. One of the ladies spotted them, and her eyes narrowed. "If you aren't a cop, why do you have those radios?"

I did not miss a beat. I told her we were communications majors in college, and those were our radios for a class project.

"Oh, ok," she said, her suspicion vanishing.

The other lady began feeling my partner's shirt, her hands searching for a mic or a wire. Since we wore our badges on a chain tucked under our shirts, I knew she felt the metal. She asked him what it was. He told her it was our school ID badges so we could work in the communications lab after hours. She looked pleased and forgot all about it. Now that they were comfortable, they both offered sex for a price. We drove a short distance and arrested them both.

What stands out to me about that incident was not the arrest—it was that instant compassion. At the time, I knew I had a "sixth sense" or a "conscience" that would alert me to "who" a person was the first time I met them. I now know that it was a gift of discernment that I have had as long as I can remember. It has kept me alive in the military and on the streets many times, though back then I usually chalked it up to "luck."

On the way to the station, I had the opportunity to speak to one of the ladies about her life choices. She told me she felt completely alone and, worse, that God was mad at her. I got to share the Gospel with her right there in the back of the patrol car. I emphasized that God is NOT mad at her—that He loves her unconditionally. She told me a heartbreaking story about how she was raised in church, but every time she made a mistake, the "religious" people would jump all over her until the shame pushed her away. Religion is such an ugly thing when it is stripped of grace; remember, it was the religious elite that persecuted and prosecuted Jesus.

The Depths of the Abyss

My heart grieved for the people I came across whose lives were being pulverized by addiction. Their decision-making was so altered, so backwards, that it broke my heart daily.

I remember one specific incident while working undercover. A woman, clearly in the throes of a heavy addiction, approached me. She looked at me with eyes that seemed to have no light left in them and said, "I will give you my nine-month-old baby girl for two rocks and a bag of burgers."

I was rocked to my core. The air felt thin. It took every ounce of my Army training and my willpower not to break my cover and scream. I had to stay the course to save that child. With all the composure I could muster, I said, "Sure, get the baby, and I'll get the burgers."

We secured the baby and arrested the woman. That little girl was so skinny, so quiet—she did not even cry. I found out later she was addicted to cocaine, having been exposed in the womb and through her environment. She was treated and eventually went to a loving foster home. I thought I knew about addiction from watching my father, but until that moment, I never knew the true, bottomless depths of that abyss.

Fight or Flight

The work was an endless cycle of use and abuse, a treadmill of human suffering that began to take its toll on my own spirit. As the work hours piled up and the darkness of the job began to seep into my bones, I fell out of my close walk with the Lord. I was not "lost," but I was living what I call a "worldly walk." I was relying on my own strength, my own discernment, and my own badge.

Then, the "green sky" returned, but this time, it did not signal a tornado. It was a diagnosis. My wife was diagnosed with terminal cancer, and in that moment, the world stopped.

The long hours had us spending more time apart than together, and it was like having a roommate you never see. All the authority of my badge and the skills of my training meant nothing. In that moment of absolute powerlessness, I reverted to my old habit: I treated God as my emergency contact. I did not know how to act or behave, and I was struggling to control the situation. I felt just like I did when I could not control losing Walker. I was a mental and spiritual wreck. In a desperate attempt to ignore the reality of the situation or downplay its severity, I began making a series of increasingly poor decisions. It was the beginning of a deep descent into a numbness I simply could not shake. I felt entirely isolated, unable to speak to anyone; I convinced myself that no one could understand the weight I was carrying.

We tried to fight. We reached back into the faith of my childhood, standing on 1 Peter 2:24: "...by whose stripes ye were healed." We repeated those words, shouting them at the darkness, claiming the miracle. We stood on that verse with everything we had...until she died.

The silence that followed was louder than any artillery boom at Fort Sill. It was a silence that demanded an answer. Why had the "Fourth Man" been in the car with me during the seven rolls, but absent from the hospital room? Why had the turkey appeared on the porch for my mother, but the healing did not appear for my wife?

I was a protector who could not protect another person I cared about, the one person who mattered most. I was a Scout who had lost the trail. As I stood numbly by her grave in the red Oklahoma dirt, I realized that my understanding of God's "will" was about to undergo a transformation as radical as the one I experienced at Fort Knox. I was about to learn that sometimes, "doing your part" means walking through the silence until you can hear the whisper of God again.

16

LOST AND FOUND

I got mad.

I did not just get angry in the way a man blows off steam after a difficult day on patrol; I became consumed by a cold, searing fury that burned through every bridge I had left. I resigned from the Lawton Police Department, handed in the badge I had once been so proud to wear, and ran.

I told God, "You don't know me. We checked every box, and you did not listen." Grief is a heavy rucksack; far heavier than the seventy-pound wet packs we carried through the frozen woods of Fort Knox. When my wife died, I did not just lose my partner, the mother of my children, and my best friend; I lost my spiritual coordinates. I lost my bearings and had no boundaries.

I looked at the "get healed" checklist we had meticulously followed—the prayers, the fasting, the constant confession of scripture—and I felt like the ultimate victim of a divine bait-and-switch. I felt like a Scout who had been given a map by his commander, followed it perfectly, and walked straight into an ambush. I was done. I was a single father to two small boys—nine and four years old—and the grueling, unpredictable hours of law enforcement, especially K-9 work and narcotics, were no longer a possibility. I could not be a police officer and a present father to two boys who had just lost the center of their universe.

So, I did the only thing I knew to do: I ran. I did not just quit; I fled. I ran as far as I could without crossing a national border, landing in Seattle—a place of gray skies and misty rain that perfectly matched the weather in my soul. It was a place where nobody knew my name, where the red dirt of Oklahoma was a thousand miles away, and where I hoped no one, including God, would bother looking for me. I settled into a corporate job with a wireless phone company, traded my Glock and my badge for a desk and engineering projects, and tried to figure out how to raise two boys on my own. My heart was a stone. I told God exactly what I thought of Him: "You don't know me. We did our part, and You did not listen. How could You know me?"

The Fragile Foundation

Returning from the theater of war in Iraq, the streets of Lawton, and too many hospitals to count, I was a man carrying a heavy, silent burden. In a desperate search for affection, consolation, and some form of pity to dull the edge of what I had been through, I ran straight into the arms of the first person who would have me. Driven by a need to feel human again, we hurried into a marriage that had no real foundation. It was a union built on hurt—a pain so deeply buried that I convinced myself no one would ever find it.

During those years, my emotions remained locked away, hidden from the world. The only thing that occasionally broke through the surface was a simmering, molten anger I felt toward God. I blamed Him for the losses I had seen and the coldness I now felt.

Unfortunately, life has a way of testing a foundation. Without a solid base of shared history or healed hearts, everything began to fall apart. The marriage could not sustain the weight of the ghosts I brought with me, and it eventually ended. Once again, I found myself broken, and the weight of the failure sat squarely on my shoulders. I viewed the divorce as just another failure to "chalk up" to the "broken protector"—a man who, in his own mind, had failed to protect the very thing he had helped build.

However, even at their absolute worst, I was blessed. Out of that difficult union came the most beautiful daughter a man could ever hope or wish for. She became the light in a very dark season, a reminder that even from a broken foundation, something perfect and lasting can grow. She was the one thing I managed to get exactly right.

The Mirror and the Shadow

The memories were a relentless, unforgiving tide, and I found myself struggling under the staggering, combined weight of the life I had lived. There was the haunting loss of Walker's death in the desert, the grief for the wife I had lost to cancer, and now, the fresh wreckage of a failed marriage.

I would go to bed, drifting into a restless sleep, only to "come to" in the dark hours of the night. I would find myself standing at the bedroom window, staring out into the void, where I saw the faces of dead, bloody soldiers. They looked at me with an intensity that pierced my soul, as if they were waiting for me to apologize or somehow explain the impossible: why they were dead and I was still alive.

In those waking nightmares, the air around me felt alive with the past. Bullets and tracers flew at me once again, zipping through the darkness as if I were the next one marked for the grave.

The VA continued to push Prozac and a cocktail of other medications on me, trying to chemically silence the deep-seated issues I had carried for years. But the pills only created a different kind of void.

Amid that medicinal fog, I found myself searching for a different kind of relief at the bottom of a bottle. For the first time in my life, I understood how alcoholism or drug addiction could look like a practical exit. It was not about the thrill; it was about the anesthesia. It was a temporary escape that stopped the crushing pain just long enough for me to catch my breath before the tide pulled me under again.

But then, a different kind of darkness moved in. I heard a voice that mimicked empathy, pretending to understand my pain while leading me toward a ledge.

"Why are you still here?" the voice hissed. "Why don't you just take the painless way out and make all this stop? Your kids will not have to suffer because of you anymore, and you will not be able to hurt anyone else in a relationship. They do not understand you anyway. Just end it all, finally. God is a just God; He will understand."

The thoughts looped endlessly as I sat on the edge of my bed, trapped in a downward spiral. Then, as if waking from a trance, I looked up at my reflection in the mirror. My heart stopped. I saw myself holding a loaded gun in my mouth.

Instantly, a second voice—sweeter and infinitely more powerful—filled my head. The same voice I had heard as a child, in the military, and as a police officer. It was quiet, yet it carried an authority that silenced the darkness. It said, "This is not for you. I have a plan for you. Your kids and others you do not even know yet need you."

The first voice, which had sounded so "reasonable" just moments before, now sounded bitter, angry, and hollow. The contrast was undeniable. I pulled the gun away, my hands shaking as I tossed it on the bed. I looked toward the ceiling and cried out, "God, I asked and asked...I thought you knew me. I need help."

It was the most honest prayer I had ever prayed—a cry for help from a protector who finally realized he could not protect himself. I was still angry and stubborn, but wanted to at least try for my kids' sake. I still was not ready to concede.

I wanted nothing to do with church and did not need anyone else telling me how badly I had messed up. I knew better than anyone how I had failed. But, in my mind, the "Emergency Contact" had failed the most important call of my life. I had dialed 911 in the spirit, and the line had gone dead. But I did not want my kids growing up like weeds. I had spent too many years as a police officer arresting "weeds" on the streets of Lawton—kids who had no direction, no foundation, and no father to tell them they were worth something. I wanted my children to have a foundation, even if I felt like my own had turned to sinking sand.

I was rocked to my core and did not think anything else could touch the deep unease I felt. I had been through the wringer and had to figure out what to do next. But just when I thought I could not be shaken any more than I had been, I was given a reminder that I was standing on ground I did not own.

The Shifting Foundation

On February 28, 2001, I was sitting in my office on the fourth floor of my corporate building in Redmond, Washington. I had transitioned into a role at AT&T Wireless Corporate as a project manager for engineering projects. Looking back, that career move was a blessing and a clear testimony of God's provision, though at the time, I was not yet in a spiritual place where I was ready to acknowledge His hand in my life.

I was kicked back in my chair, enjoying a moment of quiet as I looked out the large office windows at the sprawling Pacific Northwest landscape. I was on the phone with my brother Joe, who was back home in Oklahoma, catching up on life across the miles, when the strangest and most surreal thing began to happen.

At exactly 10:54 am Pacific Time, the world outside began to distort. As I watched, the massive glass windows started to move like water. They did not just rattle or shake in their frames; they began to move in visible waves, undulating up and down in a fluid motion.

I sat there frozen, unable to believe what my senses were reporting. I genuinely felt like my eyes were playing tricks on me. In that split second, a terrifying thought crossed my mind—the relentless pressure of the stress and the unprocessed weight of the grief I had been carrying were finally causing a complete mental breakdown. I watched the glass ripple, waiting for reality to snap back into place or for the world to fall apart.

I stood up and watched for about 30 seconds as the glass looked more like liquid than a solid. Then I heard it. It started as a low, guttural rumble, like a freight train—the same sound I had heard in the storm cellar in 1979—and it grew louder as I felt the entire four-story building start to sway. Not a vibration, but a massive lean to the left, then the right. I realized this must be what an earthquake feels like. I shouted into the phone to my brother, "We are having an earthquake!" and hung up.

Being from Oklahoma, where the ground is usually as steady as a rock (aside from the occasional tornado), I had no idea what the protocol was. I stood there, mesmerized by the swaying of the concrete and steel. I watched colleagues who were "earthquake savvy" at once dive under desks or run to gather in the reinforced doorways. They were screaming at me to get into a doorway, but I was a Scout— my instinct was to move, to find an exit. I looked at the doorway, looked at the stairs, looked at the doorway, and then I bolted.

I ran down four flights of stairs in record time, my heart hammering like a machine gun, and burst out into the middle of the street. But there was no safety there. The ground itself was rolling in visible waves. All the buildings around me were moving back and forth like trees in a high wind. I had never seen anything like it. In the military, during combat or high-stakes police operations, you at least have a sense of the "front." There is an "over there" where the danger is. But with this earthquake, it was sudden, spontaneous, and all-consuming. There was nowhere to run because the very earth you were standing on had turned into an enemy. No storm shelter, no armored vehicle... it was everywhere.

After about a minute — the whole episode lasted less than three minutes — it felt like a lifetime: everything got deathly quiet. I stood in the street, stunned. I had never felt so helpless and so small. I knew instantly how little control I had.

I realized I had been trying to build a new life entirely on my own strength, and the earth had just reminded me that my strength was nothing more than dust. I was still mad, still bitter, but I had a sudden, terrifyingly clear understanding that I needed help beyond my own intellect.

That event is known as the Nisqually Earthquake. It was a 6.8 magnitude quake felt from Idaho to Canada, causing billions in damage and injuring over 400 people.

As I looked at the cracked pavement and the shaken faces around me, I realized I did not want my kids to ever feel as helpless and alone as I did. I did not want them growing up without direction, yet I was not sure I could direct anyone anywhere while I was still lost in the woods of my own resentment.

The Encounter

The pressure to provide some kind of spiritual foundation for my children eventually outweighed my desire to avoid God. I found a church in the enormous Seattle Yellow Pages and developed what I thought was a foolproof, "low-engagement" plan. I would drop them off at the door, let them get some "youth program" goodness—moral stories and goldfish crackers—and then I would pick them up and leave. I would fulfill my duty as a father without having to face the Commander I was so bitter toward.

The plan hit a snag the moment I stepped inside. The children's pastor informed me that, because it was their first time and for security reasons, I had to stay on-site. I could not just "drop and run."

Feeling trapped, I wandered into the sanctuary. It was massive—at least 600 to 700 people were packed into the room. I felt a surge of relief at the size of the crowd. I found a seat two rows from the very back, right in the middle of a massive forty-person pew. I was a needle in a haystack, a face in the crowd, and that was exactly how I wanted it. I was there in body, but my heart was behind a reinforced wall.

I sat through the sermon with my arms crossed over my chest, physically guarding my heart. I was half-heartedly hoping for a revelation—some bolt of lightning to explain why my life had been dismantled—but the sermon did not move me. I felt nothing. When the service ended, the congregation stood to let the pastor exit. He was walking down the center aisle, surrounded by his wife and a small security team.

As he walked, passing hundreds of people, he suddenly stopped. He was just past my row when he paused, looked back, and backed up to my pew. He looked deep into the row, past the lengthy line of people, directly at me. He whispered something to one of his security guys and then kept walking.

I shook my head, my old police skepticism rising. There is no way he was looking at me, I thought. Not with all these people. Not with me hidden in the back. "God, you still don't know me," I muttered to myself as I started shuffling through the maze of people toward the exit.

I reached the lobby, but standing there, blocking my path with the quiet authority of a man on a mission, was one of the security guys I had seen earlier. He looked me in the eye and said, "The pastor would like a word with you."

"You have the wrong guy," I said, my voice sharp. "I've never been here. I have never even been to Seattle until recently. He doesn't know me."

"He just wants a quick word," the man repeated, already turning to lead the way.

I followed him hesitantly toward the office area in the back of the church. My mind was spinning with cynicism. He saw the new guy and wants a donation, I told myself. Or he wants to recruit me for a committee. I was angry, hurt, and ready for a fight. I walked into the office and saw the pastor and his wife, along with a few others, and the security team.

The pastor looked at me with a kindness that felt intrusive. "Is this your first time here?" he asked.

"Yes," I replied shortly. "I've never been to Seattle before."

"The Lord highlighted you to me," he said, his voice dropping to a serious, steady tone. "And He wants me to tell you something."

The hairs stood up on the back of my neck, and my palms were instantly sweaty. It was the same feeling I had in the desert before a firefight—that sudden, electric awareness that everything was about to change. Hope and unbelief battled in my chest as I managed to squeak out a quiet, "Okay."

He looked right at me, pinning me with a gaze that felt like it was reading my very soul. "The Lord wanted me to tell you He DOES know you. And He has been with you through the whole process you are walking through."

The air left the room. It felt like the earthquake had returned, but this time it was my internal world that was shaking. The stone in my chest did not just crack; it shattered.

"You don't know me," I managed to whisper through the tears that were suddenly, uncontrollably welling up. "You can't know what I've been through."

"You're right," the pastor said softly. "I don't. But God does. He also wants me to tell you He is preparing you to speak His word to many, many people, and He wants to let you know He is walking beside you."

I was stunned. The "Emergency Contact" I had been ignoring had not just taken my call—He had hunted me down. I barely remember saying "thank you" or "goodbye." I walked out of that office in a daze, tears streaming down my face. I had run thousands of miles to tell God He did not know me, only for Him to find me in a forty-person pew in a city where I was a stranger, just to tell me He had never lost sight of me.

I never went back. I was not ready to fully surrender yet; the pride of a Scout and the hardness of a police officer are not easily broken. But the message had been delivered. The Commander had refused my resignation. He was telling me that my "process"—the grief, the anger, the running—was not a detour; it was part of the training.

The Call of the Red Dirt

In the weeks that followed, I started to question God more—not with the "why" of bitterness, but with a desperate "how." How was I supposed to move forward? How was I supposed to be the man He was calling me to be?

I began to feel a pull that I could not ignore. It was the pull of the red dirt. I received word from Oklahoma that my dad was not doing very well. His years of "drowning the voice" had taken their toll on his body.

I realized it was time to head back home. I needed to seek direction and also close the loop with my father. I needed to see the man who had been a ghost in my childhood before he became a literal one. I packed up the kids and the fragments of my life in Seattle and began the long drive back toward the Wichita Mountains. I did not have all the answers, but for the first time since my wife died, I was not running from something. I was moving toward something.

The Scout was returning to the original terrain, realizing that you cannot truly find your way home until you admit that you were never really lost to the One who made you.

17

THE BROKEN PROTECTOR

I moved back to Oklahoma with a singular goal: to find a place where I could breathe without the weight of my past pressing against my lungs. I chose Oklahoma City, a sprawling metro that offered enough anonymity to provide some peace from the streets I had policed. In Lawton, every street corner was a memory, and every restaurant was a potential confrontation. I never knew who I would run into—someone I had arrested in a drug raid or written a heavy ticket to—while I was trying to eat a quiet meal with my kids or shop for groceries. I needed a fresh start, a neutral ground where the "Officer" did not have to exist unless I chose to let him out.

I enrolled at Oklahoma City University to finish my master's degree and start on my doctorate. I decided to sharpen my mind for whatever civilian chapter lay ahead. To provide for us, I fell back on the ability I had mastered in both the military and law enforcement: firearms instruction. I was a certified instructor, but my philosophy went deeper than just hitting a bullseye. I focused on the "Scout" mentality—teaching people not just to shoot, but to handle a weapon with respect and safety.

Little did I know, the range would be the site of a different kind of "targeting." A mutual friend introduced me to Rebekah. I was instantly smitten. She was smart, beautiful, and as it turned out, an excellent shot! She had a strength that matched my own and a grace that challenged my cynicism. She was the one. But I had been through the fire; I knew to take things slowly, for the sake of my heart, two boys who were still healing from the loss of their mother, and a sweet little girl.

Returning to Oklahoma, however, meant more than just a new career and a new love. It meant facing the one man who stood for my earliest memories, my deepest hurts, and my most haunting questions.

The Ghost at the Table

My father's health was failing, and watching his decline was a strange, sobering experience. Even though he had always been a thin man, he was as tough as a boot—a hardness forged in the lean years of his youth. He was born just outside of Stonewall, Oklahoma, a blip on the map in the south-central part of the state, just southeast of Ada.

He grew up poor, coming of age in an era where survival meant backbreaking work. He spent a sizable part of his early life picking cotton under the unrelenting sun and even working as a sharecropper. After serving a short stint in the Army, he eventually found his niche as a house painter—a trade he mastered long before he met my mother and started a family.

Painting was his life's work, but it came with a heavy physical price. Over the decades, he survived at least three broken backs resulting from various accidents and falls from ladders. These injuries left his spine permanently crooked, a physical map of the falls he had taken, and caused him to lose some of his original 6'2" stature. Despite the pain, he stayed remarkably strong and capable whenever he was sober; he was a man who seemed to truly thrive on the demands of manual labor.

However, the internal damage was just as severe as the external. He was eventually diagnosed with cirrhosis of the liver and was forced to have a part of his stomach removed. I vividly remember the doctor's blunt warning to my mother: if Dad took another drink, he would not survive. Yet his body stubbornly ignored medical advice. He continued his cycle of off-and-on drinking binges for years.

The Fragile Giant

It was not just the alcohol that took a toll; it was the trade itself. Decades of heavy drinking combined with his habit of using harsh paint thinner to scrub the paint from his face and hands eventually contributed to an aggressive form of skin cancer. This was the one thing that finally slowed him down.

The treatment was nothing short of brutal. Surgeons were forced to remove his soft palate, one eye, and a part of his jaw to stop the spread of the disease. The man who had once been a towering, if distant, figure of my childhood—a man defined by a signature scent of cheap beer, fresh paint, and the medicinal sting of Icy Hot—was very fragile. The toughness remained in his spirit, but the frame that carried it was finally reaching its limit.

He was limited to eating only soft foods and speaking in a calculated, soft, labored voice that required me to lean in close, inches from his face, to hear him. It was a physical manifestation of the vulnerability he had spent a lifetime trying to hide.

Because he could only eat soft food, his meals became slow, deliberate rituals. For the first time in my life, the "ghost" was forced to be still. The chronic alcoholic, the one we could never count on to provide or protect us, the one who had been a whirlwind of instability, was finally quiet. We sat at his kitchen table for hours. The air was no longer filled with the thick tension of his drinking or the looming threat of an outburst. Instead, it was filled with the heavy, vibrating silence of things left unsaid for thirty years.

It was during these one-on-one conversations that the armor finally came off. I looked at my father, and I did not see the man who had failed to fix the drafty house in Lawton. I did not see the man who had been absent for Christmases. I saw a man whose eyes held the same haunted, hollow look I had carried in mine after Walker was killed and my wife died. It was the look of a man who had failed to protect what he loved most and had spent the rest of his life punishing himself for it.

This was when he finally told me about Ronnie.

The 1957 Tragedy

He took me back to that day in 1957. He described the sterile, cold feeling of the hospital waiting room. He recounted the routine surgery that was supposed to be a simple fix but instead turned into a nightmare. He described holding his five-year-old son, watching the life drain out of him as the bleeding would not stop. He described how he wanted to kill the doctor who botched the surgery. He wept as he recounted Ronnie's pleas: "It hurts, please make it stop, Daddy."

For my father, that moment was the end of his world. He had stood there, a grown man, a father, a protector, and he had been utterly powerless. All his strength could not stop the bleeding. All his love could not keep his son on this earth.

I looked at my father, and the revelation hit me like a physical blow. I did not see a "falling-down drunk" anymore. I saw a broken protector. He had not been drinking because he loved the bottle; he had been drinking because he was trying to drown out the sound of a five-year-old's voice. He had been running from that memory for thirty years, and he had finally run out of road.

As we spoke, the depth of my father's shame finally came to the surface. He spoke with a trembling honesty about the suffering his addiction had inflicted upon us—the freezing cold nights when the utilities were turned off, the humble gifts wrapped in old newspaper, and the immense, silent burden my mother had been forced to carry alone. He honestly believed he was beyond the reach of the very grace I had just rediscovered in Seattle. In his mind, God was not a loving Father who had received his son, Ronnie, but a vengeful Judge who had taken him away as punishment.

He confessed that he had tried to quit before. He had even tried to return to church, but the harshness of the "Christians" he met had only made him feel more condemned.

Then, it hit me. Like a white-hot knife to the heart, a memory surfaced, and I remembered exactly when the door to his faith had been slammed shut.

A Miracle on Father's Day

I had never seen my dad in church, but on one specific Father's Day, the impossible happened. I will never forget the electric feeling in the house as we shared space in our tiny bathroom, all of us getting prepared for the service together. He was going with us. I was a whirlwind of excitement and mystification.

Dad put on his absolute best—a sharp "Brushpopper" shirt, his cleanest jeans, and his cowboy boots. He crowned the look with his cowboy hat, standing tall while Mom worked Brylcreem into our hair to ensure we looked our best. We drove to the church as a family—a rare, unified front. When we walked in, we took up five spaces in a single pew.

I had never sat higher in my life. I was so overwhelmed with pride that, for the first time in my life, I wanted church to last longer. I could see how nervous Dad was, his hands wringing in his lap, but I could also see the quiet pride he felt having his entire family gathered in the house of God.

The Unkindness of the "Righteous"

I strained my ears, expecting to hear the congregation whisper about how wonderful it was to see him, or how proud they were of our family. I waited for the compliments to flow freely and steadily. Instead, the words I heard broke my heart and changed my father's life forever.

The women within earshot did not whisper; they unleashed.

"How could that man even step foot in this church after all the pain he caused that family?" "He is going to burn in hell for what he has done." "I'm surprised he hasn't burst into flames yet." "What is THAT MAN doing here?" "That is no man; he is worse than an infidel."

I watched the color drain from my father's face until he was as white as a sheet. He began to sweat profusely, the weight of their judgment becoming a physical burden he could not carry. Without a word, he stood up, walked out of the church, and never returned.

When we got home after the service, I remember the air in the house was heavy. I overheard Mom talking to him, trying to bridge the gap, but Dad's heart had turned to stone. He spoke bitterly about hypocrites and declared it would be a "cold day in hell" before he ever darkened the door of a church again.

That day, as a young boy, I learned a devastating lesson in biblical grace and mercy. I saw firsthand what happens when those virtues are withheld from the very people who need them most. It took decades of life, a war, and a near-death experience for me to realize that those voices in the pews were not the voice of God—and even longer to convince my father of the same.

.   .   .

The Final Mission

My mission suddenly became clear. My purpose was not to act as a judge of his past or to read aloud the lengthy list of his failures; I was there to stand in the gap for his future. I was the eyes and ears in that room, and I could see the light on the horizon even if he was still lost in the shadows. I looked at this man—this man who had shaped the very fabric of my world through both his presence and his painful absences—and I did the only thing that had the power to break the cycle of generational hurt.

I looked him in the eye and told him I forgave him.

I told him I loved him. But more importantly, I told him that God was not mad at him. I explained that my brother Ronnie was safe and waiting, and that the "Fourth Man" who stood in the fiery furnace with Shadrach, Meshach, and Abednego—the same One who had been with me in the wreckage of the car accident and whom I had finally found in the sands of the Iraqi desert—was the very same One waiting to walk him home.

As those words settled, I watched a genuine smile break across his face. It was a rare, beautiful sight—a flash of the man he was meant to be—that even the deep scars of his surgery and the missing part of his jaw could not diminish. It was a smile of pure liberation. In that moment, he was living out the truth of grace and mercy.

Chipping Away the Facade

I was not alone in this mission. My brothers and sisters all did what they could, but I remember my brother Joe and the countless hours he spent driving our father back and forth from Lawton to Oklahoma City for his medical appointments. Joe used every mile of those long trips to minister to him, patiently planting seeds of grace that began to chip away at the rough, stony facade my father had perfected over decades of shame and regret.

I was thankful that I had been given a few small windows of time to do the same. Because of those moments, when the end finally came shortly thereafter, he did not leave this world as a ghost of his former self, a drunk, or a failure. He left as a redeemed man who had finally found peace with his Creator and his son.

Doing My Part

I realized then that the "protector" mission is not just about wearing badges, blowing things up, or carrying a weapon. It is about standing in the gap for the broken. It is about being a shepherd for those who have lost the trail. It is about being willing to walk back into the "red dirt" of someone else's life—no matter how messy or stained it is—to tell them they are not forgotten, and they are not beyond saving.

God had strategically placed everyone in my path to ensure I reached this moment of clarity. He used my mother's prayers to keep me alive until age twelve and beyond. He used Phil and Darlene to show me what a stable home felt like. He used the drill sergeants to show me I could endure. He even used a Seattle pastor and an earthquake to shake me out of my bitterness.

God did His part. He provided the manna, the protection, and the mercy.

Now, with a new partner by my side and a heart that has been mended from the inside out, I am finally ready to do mine. I am no longer just a Scout looking for the enemy; I am a Scout looking for the hurting, ready to lead them toward the light.

18

THE DIVINE SETUP

As I settled into the rhythm of life in Oklahoma City, the world felt like it was finally finding equilibrium. I was no longer hyper-vigilant, scanning the horizon for the next "green sky" or the next roadside ambush. I was a father, a student, a firearms instructor, and a man trying to reconcile the fractured pieces of his past with the quiet potential of his future. Yet, despite the peace, that word from the Seattle pastor began to itch at the back of my mind like a physical sensation.

I was, by training and by nature, a person of action. If a Scout is given a destination, he does not just sit and wait for a helicopter to drop him there; he begins searching for the trail. I started searching for understanding. I needed to know how to speak, and more importantly, I needed to know exactly what I was supposed to say. I knew the "Lawton" version of God—the one who provided turkeys and nuts in socks—, and I knew the "Emergency Contact" version of God, whom I called upon when the car started flipping. But I realized I did not truly know the character of God. I needed the truth, unvarnished and stripped of the religious traditions that had pushed my father (and so many others I met) away from the light.

The Gospel on the Screen

One afternoon, I found myself doing something I rarely had the patience for: flipping aimlessly through television channels. I have always been deeply skeptical of "TV preachers." To me, they felt like a distraction—a polished, synthetic veneer of spirituality cluttered with commercial interruptions and high-pressure sales pitches. They were constantly peddling "anointed oil" or "blessed cloths," delivering performances that felt more like a Hollywood production than a move of the Holy Spirit.

None of it aligned with the grind of the life I had lived. I had seen too much blood on the pavement and too much dirt in the trenches to be moved by a man in a three-thousand-dollar suit telling me that a "seed" of money would solve all my problems. My faith was forged in fire, not in a studio.

The church I grew up in was a world entirely different from the one I live in now. It was a Pentecostal congregation defined by raw, unfiltered emotion—loud praying, intense crying, and people running up and down the aisles in a fervor. As a child, I quickly grew used to the chaos, but I remember that whenever we brought a friend, they were usually terrified by the sheer volume and intensity of the service.

Easy Lessons

I will never forget the earliest memory I have of "discernment." I was only eight years old, but I had already given my heart willingly to the Lord. I loved Jesus with a pure, uncomplicated trust; nothing in my short life compared to the sense of joy and peace that came with that commitment.

Shortly after my conversion, we were in a service when a woman a few pews over began shouting at the top of her lungs, crying out with an ear-piercing volume. As I watched her, I felt a sharp "check" inside my spirit. Even at eight, I knew instinctively that what she was doing was not real. I grabbed my mom's arm, and as she leaned down, I whispered, "Mom, that's not real."

She looked over at the woman, then back down at me with a look of serious validation. "Yes," she said quietly. "Don't you ever forget that. People will try to bring attention to themselves."

In that moment, God was teaching me how to hear His still, small voice, and I had enough of the "faith of a child" to believe exactly what I was hearing. Instantly, my focus shifted to another woman sitting directly in front of me. She was also praying aloud and crying loudly, but the feeling in my spirit was the complete opposite.

INSTANTLY, I felt a supernatural peace. I knew without a doubt that her worship was authentic; she was truly rejoicing and communing with the Lord. I took that lesson with me for the rest of my life, using that "still small voice," that inexplicable peace, and that gift of discernment through the war, on the streets as a police officer, and in my own living room.

The Tractor Beam of Truth

As I continued flipping through the channels, skeptical as ever, I landed on a specific station and stopped. My finger hovered over the remote, poised to move on to the next distraction, but the skepticism that usually guarded my heart like a reinforced gate met something entirely unexpected.

The show was called The Gospel Truth, hosted by Andrew Wommack. It did not look like much—certainly, nothing like the high-production spectacles I usually avoided. It was just a man sitting in a chair, talking directly to the camera as if he were sitting across a kitchen table. But within thirty seconds, I realized this was different. There was no fluff. There was no theatrical yelling, no emotional manipulation, and no frantic plea for money. Instead, it was as if I were being drawn into the screen by a tractor beam of pure, logical, and biblical clarity.

Every word Andrew spoke hit me with the force of a physical strike, cutting through the thick, calcified layers of cynicism I had built up over years of dealing with law enforcement, death, and war. My career had taught me to look for the "angle," the hidden motive, and the lie. But here, for the first time in a long time, the "still small voice" of discernment I had learned as an eight-year-old boy was silent, replaced by a calming sense of peace.

He spoke about the grace of God not as a "maybe" or a "perhaps," but as a finished work. He spoke about a God who was not angry or waiting to strike us down, but a Father who was madly in love with us. Everything he said had a scriptural reference, not just "the Bible says" or "somewhere in the Bible" stock answers.

The most incredible part of the experience was the precision of his message. He was addressing the very things I had been secretly praying about in the deep quiet of my own home—questions of identity, worth, and purpose that I had not even voiced to my brothers or my closest friends. It was as if God had shone a celestial spotlight on this man specifically for me, using him as a spiritual Scout to map out the territory I was truly supposed to occupy.

The Convergence of Two Paths

As I continued to watch The Gospel Truth regularly, I found myself increasingly hungry for more of that message. I later learned that Andrew Wommack had a Bible college in Colorado, and I developed an "itch" to move there if possible. The practical planning was a mountain I did not know how to climb. I was a single father with two young boys and a daughter who depended on me for everything, and I was right in the middle of completing my master's degree. The "Scout" in me looked at the map of my life and saw a thousand obstacles between the plains of Oklahoma and the peaks of the

Rockies. But I was starting to realize that the same God —the one who had walked with me through the Iraqi desert and the wreckage of my truck—was meticulously clearing a path for a new mission.

While my spirit was being fed through the television screen, my heart was being mended in the natural world. Rebekah and I had started dating regularly, and our relationship felt like the collision of two people who had finally found the same frequency.

Seeking the Foundation

Rebekah was coming out of a difficult marriage of her own, with two small boys. Like me, she moved with extreme caution. We were two people who had been through the fire and were exceedingly careful not to get burned again. We spent hours talking—not just about our pasts, but about our hopes. We shared a common language of discipline, resilience, and faith. She understood my deep-seated need to protect, and I understood her need for a steady, reliable partner to safeguard her heart. We sought the Lord's guidance at every step, unwilling to move unless we felt His peace.

One day, while Rebekah was away on vacation, she called me. I could hear a palpable spark of excitement in her voice—a lightness and a joy that made me smile before she even said a word.

"Turn it on Channel 25," she said, her voice brimming with anticipation. "Right now. I want you to see something."

I walked over to the TV and flipped the channel. To my absolute surprise, the familiar face of Andrew Wommack filled the screen. He was right in the middle of teaching the very principles of grace and the finished work of Christ that had been transforming my mind for months.

"Hey! I love this show," I told her, genuinely stunned that she even knew who he was. "I watch him all the time. He really speaks to me. Do you watch this also?"

There was a long pause on the other end of the line. Then, she laughed—the kind of laugh that knows a secret you are about to find out, a laugh that sounded like a "divine setup" coming to fruition.

"Yes!" she said, the joy finally spilling over. "Andrew Wommack is my uncle!"

The man I had been watching in secret, the man whose college I was "toying" with the idea of attending, was the uncle of the woman I was falling in love with. It was another message from God: the mission was a go, the path was clear, and the Scout was no longer working alone.

The Ultimate Strategist

"Wait... what?"

The word hung in the air, barely more than a whisper. I was stunned. I sank onto the edge of my sofa, the phone pressed hard against my ear, my mind racing to find a response that did not exist. The odds were astronomical—beyond anything I could calculate. I was just a kid from Lawton, an Army veteran, and a former police officer living in Oklahoma City. I had been watching a man on a television screen in Colorado who was slowly transforming my spiritual life, only to discover that I was dating his niece.

After we talked for a few more minutes about the sheer impossibility of the "coincidence," we hung up. The room went completely still. The sudden silence was so heavy that the low hum of the refrigerator felt like a roar. I sat there in the quiet, stunned by the weight of the realization. The woman I was falling for—the woman I had met at a gun range, a place that felt like home to me—was the flesh-and-blood niece of the man God was using to mentor me from a distance.

I looked up at the ceiling and spoke into the empty room. "God... what are you doing?"

· · ·

The One who sees

It was a question, but as the seconds passed and I looked deeper at the map of my life, I realized I already knew the answer. He was doing what He had always done: acting as the ultimate Strategist. He was meticulously placing the right people in the right positions at the exact right time, using a level of precision that my mind could finally appreciate.

I saw the patterns clearly now. He had used a gun range to introduce me to my partner, recognizing that I needed someone who shared my passion for protection and understood the weight of the sheepdog's life. Then, He had used a television screen to introduce me to a spiritual mentor I so desperately needed, knowing my cynicism required the truth to be delivered with the same blunt directness I had used during my years in the military. He was speaking my language.

The Hand of God was leading me. For the first time in my life, I was not just following orders out of fear, habit, or a grim sense of duty. I was following a father who cared about the smallest, most intricate details of my happiness. I had spent a lifetime looking for the enemy over the next ridge, but now, I was finally looking at the One who had cleared the path before I even knew it existed.

A Direction Home

I can see now that every chapter of my life was part of a meticulously crafted "Divine Setup." The terrifying "green sky" of the 1979 Lawton tornado, the bone-chilling November rain of Fort Knox, the seven violent rolls of my truck in the Mojave Desert, and the black-smoke oil fires of Iraq—none of it was accidental. Even the personal "earthquakes" of my life—the devastating stab of Walker's death, the chaotic silence following my wife's passing, the literal earthquake in Seattle, and the dark, dangerous alleys of Lawton where I served as a police officer—were not wasted moments of suffering. Instead, they were opportunities for growth as I prepared for the next steps in my walk. God did not cause the bad but used the opportunities for good.

The pain was not just pain; it was the "red dirt" that provided the necessary friction I needed to grow, to gain traction, and to become the man I am today. The losses were not merely exits or endings; they were the clearing of the landscape, the demolition of a fragile foundation so that God could build something permanent, something eternal.

From Survivor to Witness

I realized that the words spoken by the Seattle pastor years ago were not just a prediction of things to come; they were a formal assignment. I was to speak God's word because I had lived the gritty, unvarnished reality of God's deliverance. I was not just a "survivor" who had managed to outrun the storms of life; I was a witness to the One who commands the wind and the waves. I had seen the "Fourth Man" in the furnace, and now I had the scars to prove He was real.

I am no longer the "broken protector" sitting at a kitchen table haunted by the ghost of what used to be. I am a man standing in the full, unadulterated light of the Gospel Truth. I still carry the identity of the Cavalry: I have my Stetson, I have my Spurs, and I have my Shield of Faith. The equipment has simply been upgraded for the ultimate theater of operations.

The Mission Ahead

God did His part. He stayed with me through the valley of the shadow of death when I was half-out of a truck window in the desert. He found me in the back of the church when I was an "infidel" unworthy of His grace. He brought me back to the red dirt of my home to find the peace that had eluded me for so long.

Now, with Rebekah by my side—my partner, my best friend, and the niece of the man who helped lead me to the truth—I am finally and fully back on mission. Together, with our blended family of five children, we have a clear path ahead. The reconnaissance is over. The terrain has been mapped. The scout has finally found his direction home.

Mom Gets Her Reward

As the years pressed on, Mom began a slow, quiet decline into the fog of memory loss. The woman who had been our family's unwavering architect of faith started to lose the blueprints of her own daily life. Jackie and Debbie—the steady pillars they had always been—moved her into their home to keep watch. In her confusion, Mom would often wander, trying to drive or walk "home" to a past that no longer existed, only to be found along the highway, searching for a landmark only she could see.

Eventually, the difficult decision was made to move her into assisted living. Though the details of the world around her were fading, her spirit remained constant; she would always offer a radiant smile— that same light she had reflected her entire life—the moment one of us walked into the room.

When her breathing grew shallow and labored, the doctor called us in for the final watch. We gathered around her bed, a family forged in the red dirt and refined by the storms, watching the woman who had fought for us through every "lean year" and "loud storm." She was gasping for air, her body tense, still locked in the struggle—fighting to hold on for the sake of the children she had shielded for decades. We each took turns telling her how much we loved her, cherishing our times together and assuring her it was okay to let go.

I leaned down close, my voice steady, and spoke to the heart of the woman who had taught me where "Home" truly was. "It's okay, Mom.

You can let go. We're going to be okay. You did a great job. Go on home."

With those words, she took one last, deep breath. A single tear escaped, rolling down her cheek as the final weight of this world was lifted. The woman who had stood as our protector against poverty, addiction, and the very elements themselves was finally face-to-face with Jesus. I had seen many endings in my life, but this was a beginning. As much as my heart ached with the loss, I found a profound peace knowing she was no longer suffering in the ruins; she was finally, truly Home.

19

THE COMMAND
FROM THE THRONE

As Rebekah and I moved toward our future as husband and wife, the Bible became the compass by which we navigated our new life together. We were no longer content with a surface-level understanding of the Word. We wanted the "deep water"—the kind of spiritual depth that can only come from total immersion. We were immersing ourselves in amazing Bible teachings from Andrew Wommack, Bob Yandian, Duane Sheriff, Lance Wallnau, and many others we could find. We began taking correspondence classes through Charis Bible College, and the number of teachers in our field grew and grew. We were carving out time between work and family to study; however, the more we delved into the material, the more we realized that "long-distance" was no longer enough.

We felt a magnetic pull toward the source. We wanted to be there in person, standing in the atmosphere of the Colorado mountains, surrounded by the teachers who were helping us painstakingly reconstruct our faith from the ground up.

We did not just talk about it; we prepared for it. With great excitement, we decided to go. We were serious enough about this new mission that we made an official appointment with a realtor to list our house in Oklahoma City. We were prepared to pack up the kids, leave the familiar red dirt of Oklahoma behind once again, and head into the high country.

We were taking the practical, boots-on-the-ground steps of faith, moving in the direction we believed the Lord was leading. That was when God did what He always does: He performed a miracle of orchestration that left us speechless.

The Miracle in Oklahoma City

At the exact moment we finished our plans to sell our home, we received word that was nothing short of a divine intervention: Charis Bible College was opening a campus right here in Oklahoma City!

We were floored. The realization hit us like a wave—God had perfectly orchestrated the timing. He did not want us to move; He wanted us to plant. He had brought the "deep water" to the red dirt. We signed up at once, and instead of a thousand-mile move, we began a three-year journey of transformation right in our own backyard.

We eventually completed the full three-year program and graduated with degrees in Ministry and Ministry Leadership. But more than the ink on the paper, it was the "total immersion" that changed the trajectory of our lives. The most incredible aspect of the curriculum was its radical simplicity. In a world of complex theological debates, the only textbook we ever needed was the Holy Bible. We were not there to study manufactured opinions or historical theories about God; we learned to trust the Holy Spirit and walk according to His word.

After graduation, Rebekah and I did not just walk away with our degrees; we stayed to serve the mission that had saved us. We volunteered at Charis Oklahoma City for as long as we could, eventually stepping into leadership roles. When the original directors moved on to their next season, we were asked to take the helm and run the school. I had recently taken on a new job, so Rebekah went solo and took over the school.

To provide a steady income for our family during this transition, I took a job at a local high school teaching English and Street Law. It was a different kind of "reconnaissance," working with young people in the community, while I spent my weekends and evenings helping at the college. The students blessed us beyond words. Watching people walk through those doors carrying the same heavy "shadows" I once bore—and seeing those shadows flee as they met the Light— was nothing short of miraculous. God was doing what He always did: meticulously setting the stage for me to fulfill my calling. I was still a scout, but my terrain had shifted from the shifting sands of the desert to the fertile ground of the classroom.

The Office and the Vision

One afternoon, shortly after returning from a mission trip to Brazil that had cracked my heart wide open for the nations, I found myself alone in our home office. I was in a posture of prayer, seeking our next step. I felt that familiar "itch" for something more, a sense that a new horizon was appearing.

Then the room's atmospheric pressure changed. I had a supernatural experience that I can still feel in my bones to this day. I did not just feel a presence; I met Jesus face-to-face.

There are no words in the English language adequate to describe the gravity of His presence. I was overwhelmed by a love so pure, so intense, and so holy that my physical strength evaporated. My knees simply gave out. I fell on my face at His feet, completely undone by the weight of His glory.

Liquid Love and the Three Commands

He did not leave me on the floor. He reached down, helped me up, and pulled me into the most loving embrace I have ever experienced. It felt like "liquid love" was being poured over my head, soaking into every hidden scar: the terror of the 1979 tornado, the trauma of the car crash, losing a soldier, the deep ache of grief from my first wife's passing, a painful divorce, and every remaining ounce of resentment I had ever carried toward my father. In an instant, the debris of a lifetime was washed away.

People always ask me, "What did He look like?" I tell them the same thing every time: I remember His eyes. They were a beautiful, impossible contradiction. They were filled with a peace that passed all understanding and an absolute, unwavering love. Yet, at the very same time, there was a fierce, burning urgency in them—a fire that demanded a response.

I managed to think—, or I whispered it —"Lord, what can I do?"

Instantly, the answer was downloaded into my spirit. It was not a sound in the room, but a clear transmission to my soul. He told me He wanted unity in the Body of Christ. He wanted to see the five-fold ministry—apostles, prophets, evangelists, pastors, and teachers— restored to its full function. Then, He spoke a word three times with an emphasis that shook my very soul:

"Foundation. Foundation. Foundation."

He gave me my standing orders: Do not go looking for people; I will send them. Do not force the Spirit or try to manufacture a "move" of God. Take this step, and I will illuminate the next.

A New Mission

I am not sure how long I sat there after the vision faded, trying to absorb the magnitude of the encounter. My face was stained with tears, and my breath was coming in shallow gasps when Rebekah walked into the room. She took one look at me and knew something had shifted in the heavens. Through the tears, I told her everything.

I grabbed a pen and began writing down every detail with the urgency of a field report, determined never to let the specifics fade. We at once came into a covenant of agreement. With that divine command as our compass, we launched Crowned One Ministries and eventually planted Sanctuary OK church in Oklahoma City. The scout had finally received his permanent orders: to build a foundation ON HIM that would not shake.

Relationship vs. Religion

It is a curious thing to see how people react when you share that you have seen Jesus face-to-face. In my experience, most responses fall into two camps: they either look at you as if you have lost your mind or dismiss you entirely, putting no stock in a testimony that defies their logic. But I learned long ago in the military and in law enforcement that you do not judge a situation by the noise; you judge it by the results. The proof was not in my words; it was in the fruit.

Within a week of that supernatural encounter in the office, the phone began to ring. We received call after call from people saying, "God has put you two on our hearts, and we believe we are supposed to help you with your calling." We were overjoyed but not surprised. People were simply acting out exactly what Jesus said would happen.

Availability over Ability

Traveling down this long, winding trail from the red dirt of Lawton to the pulpit of Sanctuary OK, one truth stands taller than the peaks of the Wichita Mountains: Acts 10:34. It tells us plainly that "God is no respecter of persons." In the world's eyes, rank and status are everything, but the Father does not play favorites based on a title, a uniform, or a prestigious pedigree. He does not look at the medals on a chest or the degrees on a wall; He looks directly at the heart.

What He will do for the "famous" preacher commanding a global stage, He will do for you in the quiet of your own living room. His power is not reserved for the elite or the "spiritually polished." What He did for a flat-footed kid from Lawton—a man who struggled through the pain of war, the suffocating weight of grief, and the dark, lonely bottom of a bottle—He will do for you.

He is the God of the breakthrough, and He is looking for availability, not ability. If you are breathing, you are eligible for His grace. If you are seeking, you are a candidate for His restoration. He took my broken trail and turned it into a mission, proving that no matter how far you have wandered or how deep your scars are, the Father is ready to meet you exactly where you stand.

20

THE FINAL WATCH

Watching the sunset on the horizon of the Wichita Mountains no longer looks like a boundary; it looks like a beginning. The ominous peaks that once hemmed me in now stand as monuments to a journey that spans continents, decades, and the deepest valleys of the human soul. I am eternally thankful for my brothers and sisters who have stood by me through my highest peaks and lowest ebbs. They are all serving the Lord and are beautiful men and women of God.

I am still a scout. I am still a Protector. But now, my spearhead is the Gospel, and my shield is the faith of a man who knows that even when the physical house is gone, and the sky turns that terrifying shade of green, the Foundation of Christ stands unshakable.

Looking back, I can see the invisible thread that held every chaotic chapter together. It was not luck. It was not just physical toughness or the toughness of an Oklahoma upbringing. It was not even just the high-level training—though that training mattered deeply. It was the Hand of God, guiding a boy from a drafty, cold house in Lawton through storms he did not yet understand, preparing him to stand in places most people never want to go.

The 1979 tornado taught me the weight of loss—and what love looks like when it is covered in mud, stripped of possessions, and still refuses to quit. My mother's hands, muddied and searching through the debris of our life, were the first sermon that ever truly marked me.

The Army taught me how to push through misery, how to maintain clarity under extreme pressure, and how to keep moving forward when every nerve in my body screamed to stop. The deserts of Saudi Arabia taught me that Psalm 23 is not just poetry to be recited at funerals—it is a reality for the people who live "out front." Law enforcement taught me to see past a person's surface, to recognize the rough edges of hidden pain, and to understand how quickly a life can unravel when there is no spiritual foundation to hold it together.

The Weight of the Rucksack

Then there was the grief—a suffocating, weight heavier than any rucksack I had ever lugged through the grueling hills of Fort Knox. In the military, you are trained to account for your people, but nothing prepares you for the cost of that responsibility when things go wrong. Losing a soldier, whom I was responsible for, did not just hurt; it cut a part out of me that felt permanent. It was a wound so deep that only the touch of Jesus could eventually reach the bottom of it.

When my wife passed away, the world lost its color. I did not just lose a partner or a spouse; I lost my map. Every coordinate I had used to navigate my life was suddenly gone. I was left in a "dead space" of the soul—angry, bitter, and utterly convinced that if God existed at all, He certainly did not know me. I felt like a discarded instrument, forgotten in the aftermath of a life of service.

Running from the pain to Seattle, I thought that by putting thousands of miles between myself and the red dirt of home, I could finally silence the calling on my life and the agony in my heart. I wanted to disappear into the gray mist of the Pacific Northwest.

But the God who had been training a scout long before I ever put on a uniform—long before I even knew what the title meant—refused to let the trail go cold. He did not stop pursuing me. In the middle of my attempt to vanish, He met me. He did not come with a lecture; He came with a message. He spoke through a stranger to tell me the one thing my pain had refused to believe: *He knew me.* He had not been watching from a distance. He revealed to me that He had been right there in the Bradleys' turret during the heat of the desert. He had been in the front seat of the patrol car during the long, dangerous shifts. He had been standing in the corner of the hospital room during those final breaths. He had been with me the whole time, even when I was too blinded by tears to see Him.

The Return to the Red Dirt

When I finally turned back toward home and returned to the red dirt of Oklahoma, I had to face the "ghost" that had haunted our family for decades. Coming back allowed me to see something I was too young to understand as a boy. I looked at the memory of my father and saw a different man.

He was not just an alcoholic. He was not just a "falling-down drunk." He was a father who had never recovered from the day he could not save his own son, Ronnie. His addiction was not the root; it was the anesthetic for a wound that had never been dressed.

God did not lead me back to Oklahoma to reopen those old, sensitive wounds or to dwell on the "what ifs." He brought me back to bring closure, to extend forgiveness, and to demonstrate a mercy that surpasses human understanding. He showed me that the calling to protect does not end when you turn in your badge, hang up your uniform, or retire your spurs.

Sometimes, the fiercest battles of a man's life are not fought on a foreign battlefield or in a dark alley with a suspect. Sometimes, the most significant victories are won at a kitchen table, sitting face-to-face with the past, armed with nothing but grace.

The Fix

Then, God did what He does best: He began the work of the "Divine Setup." He did not just repair the broken pieces; He began to orchestrate a connection that only a Sovereign Hand could design. He brought Rebekah into my life, and I quickly realized she was far more than a wife or a companion. She was a partner in a divine purpose—a woman whose spirit matched the weight of the calling I had been running from.

During this season of rebuilding, God fed my hungry, weary spirit through the ministry of Andrew Wommack's *The Gospel Truth*. It was as if a fresh supply line had been opened directly to my soul. In the quiet moments of study and reflection, I was stunned by a realization that moved me to my core: nothing about my story was random.

The storms that leveled my childhood home, the heat of the Iraqi desert, the long nights in a patrol car, and even the "dead space" of my grief were not accidents of fate. God had been using those instances to prepare me. I was steel tempered by the forge, preparing my vision and my resolve for a mission that lie ahead.

Face to Face

Then came the moment that made all my questions irrelevant. Jesus met me—not as a distant historical figure or a theological concept, but face to face. In that instant, everything changed. It was not because I suddenly owned a manual with all the answers to life's mysteries; it was because I finally met the One who *is* the Answer.

The experience was beyond words, yet the message was unmistakable. I saw the urgency in His eyes—a deep, burning desire for the lost and the broken—and I felt the "liquid love" of His embrace. It was a love so thick and transformative that it washed away the last traces of Seattle's mist and the desert's grit. In the warmth of that embrace, the purpose of the storms, the deserts, the streets, and the grief finally became clear. They were all pointing toward a singular, glorious goal: Unity, Restoration, and Foundation.

I had spent a lifetime searching the horizon, but I finally found what I was looking for at the feet of the Father. The mission was no longer about survival; it was about the Message.

21

THE WATCH CONTINUES

So here I am, still standing watch. My silhouette has not changed, but my equipment has. I am no longer armed with a rifle, a badge, or armor forged of cold steel. Instead, I carry the Word of God, the living testimony of what He has done in my life, and the unwavering conviction that He is not mad at the broken. I have learned through fire and desert sand that He is not distant from the hurting. He is not intimidated by our questions, our deep-seated trauma, or the sharp edges of our anger. He is the Foundation under everything that shakes.

My Choices

I take full ownership of the path I have walked because I realize that God respected my will enough to let me choose my own way. I have seen the wreckage that comes from choosing man's way—the brokenness, the dead ends, and the wasted years. But I have also seen the spectacular restoration that comes from choosing His.

Every detour I took, every mistake I made, and every bridge I burned was the result of my own choices. I was the one at the helm. By that same token, the victories I have won and the good decisions I have made were also mine to claim. We are not pawns on a board, moved around by a distant player; we are active participants in a divine narrative. The power of that choice is yours, and it is the most significant authority you will ever exercise.

There is no greater test of free will than the moment of ultimate desperation. Having a gun in your mouth is the absolute, harrowing intersection of human autonomy and sheer, crushing hopelessness. It is the final, heavy "yes" or "no" to the very gift of existence—a moment where the power of choice is stripped down to its most raw and lethal form.

It is a valley so dark and so suffocating that most who find themselves there cannot see a single glimmer of a way out. But I stand here today as a witness to the fact that the light can still reach you, even there. I am eternally thankful that, in the middle of those shadow-drenched depths, I chose wisely. I chose life when death felt like the only logical conclusion, the only escape from the noise, and the only answer to the pain.

In that moment of absolute crisis, the words of Psalm 23:4 become more than just a comfort; they become a survival map: "Yea, though I walk through the valley of the shadow of death, I will fear no evil; for You are with me; Your rod and Your staff, they comfort me."

I realized that even when I had given up on myself, God had not. He respected my free will enough to let me hold the weapon, but His grace was sufficient to whisper a better way into the silence of my despair. If you are standing at that same intersection today, hear me as one who has been there: the choice for life is the most powerful "yes" you will ever speak. It is the decision that allows God to take the wreckage of your "no" and build a foundation for a future you cannot yet see. I chose to stay on the trail, and because I did, I discovered that the valley of the shadow is not a destination—it is only a pass you are meant to walk through.

· · ·

The Divine Blueprint for Success

God put this entire plan into place long before we were even a whisper of a thought. He designed a strategy to spread the Gospel to every soul that would listen. We must remember: God has already done His part. He continues to bless us in ways that transcend our understanding. Two thousand years ago, He sent His Son to the cross to finish the work for every one of us.

Now, the mission has been handed off. It is our turn to do our part. We are the boots on the ground. We must use our voices, our hands, and our feet to reach those who are still wandering in the "dead space," unaware of the Gospel Truth. To fulfill what God has ordained for us, we cannot remain stationary. It requires action.

I want to be unequivocally clear: God **did not** send, cause, or place any of these horrible, deadly events on me to "teach me a lesson." He is a Father of restoration, not a source of tragedy. Did those seasons test the very core of my being? Absolutely. But the beauty of the Father is that He consistently takes what was meant for evil and transforms it into a blessing—if we simply allow Him access to the wreckage (Genesis 50:20).

All too often, I hear people say, *"If it is God's will,"* as if His will for our success and healing is a mystery. That is the opposite of His heart!

As Jeremiah 29:11 declares: "For I know the plans I have for you,' declares the Lord, 'plans to prosper you and not to harm you, plans to give you a hope and a future.'"

3 John 1:2 says: "Beloved, I pray that you may prosper in all things and be in health, just as your soul prospers."

He does not engineer your destruction. He is a Father who delights in the restoration of His children. The blueprint for a victorious life is already drawn; the only requirement is that we stop fighting for control and let Him guide us.

· · ·

The Wisdom of the Gray

With gray hair of age comes the clarity of hindsight. I can look back now across the vast expanse of decades—navigating through the choking dust of the Middle East, the broken wreckage of the Oklahoma storms, and the heavy, sterile silence of the hospital rooms —and see with startling clarity the moments where I felt completely alone, unprotected, and unprovided for.

I see now, with eyes opened by grace, that I was never alone. He was right there all along, standing in the gaps I did not even know existed, holding the line when I was too exhausted to notice. But I also see my own reflection in those memories, with a raw, newfound honesty. I see clearly now that I wanted to be the architect of my own fortune. I wanted to be the one drawing the blueprints and making the high-stakes decisions without any input from Him, convinced that my own strength, my training, and my "scout" instincts were more than enough to see me through.

It took many hard, dusty miles and a mountain of unnecessary bruises, but I finally "got it." I finally realized that the Commander has the high-ground perspective I lack. He knows the right way, the best way, and the most strategic way through every situation we will ever meet. As Proverbs 3:5–6 instructs us: "Trust in the Lord with all your heart and lean not on your own understanding; in all your ways acknowledge Him, and He shall direct your paths."

Surrender is not a sign of weakness or a white flag of defeat. In the Kingdom of God, it is the ultimate advantage. It is the moment you stop fighting the terrain and start following the One who created it. By handing over the reins, you are not losing control—you are finally gaining the protection and the precision of the Divine Strategist. The path goes much more smoothly when you stop white-knuckling the steering wheel and let the Father lead the way.

To the One in the Shadows

If you have read this far and recognized your own reflection in these pages—if you have been the one living in that quiet, suffocating "dead space," carrying that immense weight of grief that feels heavier with every passing mile, or trying to silence the pain with whatever numbing agent you can find—hear me clearly:

God does know you.

He was not an absent observer during your darkest hours. He knew you in the screaming winds of the storm. He knew you in the hollow silence of your greatest loss. He knew you in the sharp, barbed edges of your bitterness, and He knows you right now in the beauty of your becoming. He is still calling people to their true purpose—not to build their own kingdoms, reputations, or worldly status, but to stand in the gap as a sentinel for others and to point the way toward the only Foundation that can never be erased.

If you are tired of the trek, if your boots are worn thin and your spirit is exhausted from the weight of a trail you were never meant to hike alone, it is time. If you are ready to stop running and finally lay down the heavy, rusted armor of the "broken protector" or the "fleeing scout," then it is time to start living the life you were fashioned for before the world ever touched you.

The extraction point is here. The path is clear. The Light shines through the fog, illuminating a way home you thought was lost forever. You do not have to get "cleaned up" to approach Him; you must stop and turn around. If you are ready to come home and trade your rucksack for His rest, you can start that conversation right now:

"Father, I come to You just as I am. I believe that Jesus Christ is Your Son, that He died for my sins, and that You raised Him from the dead. Jesus, I

confess You as my Lord and Savior. Lead me, guide me, and show me the foundation You have for my life. Amen."

My journey continues, no longer fueled by my own strength or "Scout" instincts, but rooted deeply in that unshakable Foundation. I am still standing watch, but I do so with the peace of a man who knows the War is already won. If you are willing, your new mission—your real life—can begin today.

ACKNOWLEDGMENTS

I am deeply grateful to those who stood in the gap and helped bring this story from the shadows into the light.

To my loving wife, Rebekah: Thank you for your unwavering support and for believing in this book—and in me—even during those long seasons when I truly thought there was no story left to tell. When the ink ran dry and the memories felt too heavy to carry, you remained my constant.

Your encouragement was the wind in my sails when I felt hopelessly becalmed in the "dead space" of my own journey. You didn't just witness the writing of these pages; you provided the grace and the strength that made the writing possible. Thank you for helping me find the words again.

To my family: Without your unwavering support, your shared memories, and your invaluable input, the map of these stories would be incomplete. You are the keepers of the chapters I was too young to remember and the witnesses to the ones I could never forget.

Thank you for helping me piece together the intricate lineage of our family and for honoring the lessons of our life together—from the red dirt of Oklahoma to the shadows of the Wichita Mountains. This book is as much a part of our collective heritage as it is my own, and I am grateful for the strength of the bonds that held us together through every season.

To Andrew Wommack: Thank you for being strategically placed in my life at exactly the moment I needed a navigator. In a season where I felt adrift and uncertain of my direction, your teaching served as the steady compass that helped guide me back onto the true path God had laid out for me. Your commitment to the Word provided the clarity I needed to silence the noise of the world and refocus on the mission the Lord had intended for me from the beginning. Thank you for your ministry and for being a vessel of the truth that led me home.

To the Pastor in Seattle: thank you for your obedience to the Lord. That one moment of listening to the Spirit was the wake-up call I desperately needed.

Finally, to the One who sees and who knew me in the storm and the desert: You were there when the green sky turned to fury, and You were there in the silent, scorched places of my life when I felt most alone. Thank you for being the immovable, eternal Foundation that cannot be erased—not by time, not by grief, and not by the shadows I tried to hide in. You are the Architect of my story and the Ground beneath my feet; thank you for bringing the scout home to the solid rock of Your grace.

ABOUT THE AUTHOR

Born the "caboose" of eight children in the heart of Southwestern Oklahoma into abject poverty and an alcoholic father, S.E. Cunningham's life has been defined by the rugged landscapes of the Wichita Mountains and a calling to protect. A veteran 19D Cavalry Scout and former law enforcement officer, he has spent decades operating in the "dead spaces" of the world—from the deserts of Iraq to the front lines of law enforcement.

After a series of profound personal losses and a wilderness journey that took him far from his roots, he experienced a radical spiritual awakening that brought him back to his true Foundation.

Today, he writes and speaks to encourage others to lay down their rusted armor and embrace the life they were fashioned for before the world touched them.

He lives in Oklahoma City, Oklahoma with his wife, Rebekah

SE-Cunningham.com

UNTITLED

The author somewhere in the desert.

Soldiers of Bravo Troop, 4th Squadron, 7th Cavalry with a captured BMP in the newly liberated Kuwait. The author is second from the left. (Standing)

PFC Charles Scott Walker
(Last picture of Walker taken with the authors' disposable camera
days before killed while on patrol.)

These pictures are of the authors parents just after the tornado
destroyed their house on April 10th, 1979. (Photos courtesy of The
Lawton Constitution)

More pictures of the author's home after the deadly tornado on April 10th, 1979, in Lawton, Oklahoma. (Photos courtesy of The Lawton Constitution)

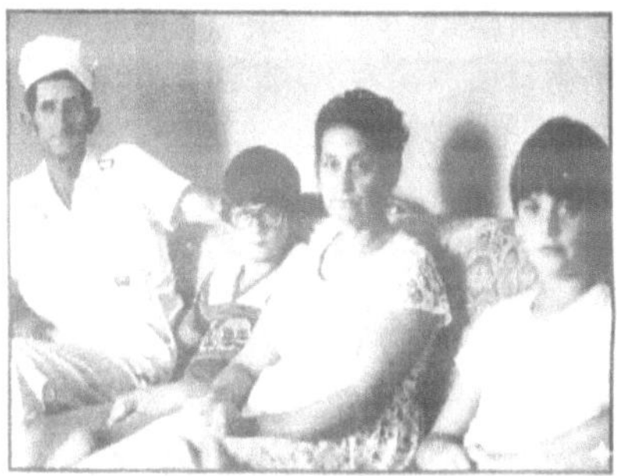

Picture of the author's dad, brother Billy, mom, and the author one year after the April 10th, 1979, tornado destroyed their home. (Photo courtesy The Lawton Constitution)